Discovering the True Riches of Life

Discovering the True Riches of Life

Todd M. Fink

Discovering the True Riches of Life

by
Todd M. Fink

Published by Selah Book Press

Cover Illustration Copyright © 2016 by Selah Book Press
Cover design by Selah Book Press

Copyright © 2016 by Todd M. Fink

ISBN-10: 1-944601-10-4
ISBN-13: 978-1-944601-10-2

First Edition

All rights reserved. No part of this publication may be reproduced or transmitted in any form or by any means, electronic or mechanical, including photocopy, recording, or any information storage retrieval system, without permission in writing from the copyright owner.

All Scripture references are taken from the English Standard Version of the Bible unless otherwise noted.

The Holy Bible, English Standard Version® (ESV®)
Copyright © 2001 by Crossway,
a publishing ministry of Good News Publishers.
All rights reserved.
ESV Text Edition: 2007

The Holy Bible, New International Version®, NIV® Copyright © 1973, 1978, 1984, 2011 by Biblica, Inc.® Used by permission. All rights reserved worldwide.

The Holy Bible, New King James Version®. Copyright © 1982 by Thomas Nelson, Inc. All rights reserved.

Scripture quotations taken from the New American Standard Bible®,
Copyright © 1960, 1962, 1963, 1968, 1971, 1972, 1973, 1975, 1977, 1995 by The Lockman Foundation
Used by permission. (www.Lockman.org)

The NET Bible®, New English Translation (NET) Scripture quoted by permission. Quotations designated (NET) are from the NET Bible® copyright ©1996-2006 by Biblical Studies Press, L.L.C.

Scripture in bold is emphasis added by the author.

ABBREVIATIONS

ESV	English Standard Version
NIV	New International Version
NKJV	New King James Version
NASB	New American Standard Bible
NET	New English Translation

Table of Contents

Introduction x

Chapter 1: The Question of All Questions 1

Chapter 2: What Are You Seeking in Life? 9

Chapter 3: Being Right with God 17

Chapter 4: Our Works and Service for Christ 45

Chapter 5: The Transformation of Our Nature 61

Chapter 6: Our Faith in God 77

Chapter 7: Our Knowledge of God 89

Chapter 8: Our Relationships 103

Chapter 9: Godly Character 127

Chapter 10: Godly Attitudes 135

Chapter 11: Spiritual Maturity 141

Chapter 12: The Cost of the True Riches of Life 147

Bibliography 163

About the Author 166

Connect with Todd (Mike) 167

Look for More Books by Todd (Mike) 169

Introduction

My family and I have been involved in mission work in Mexico since 1994. The main focus of our ministry (GoMissionsToMexico.com) is to host short-term mission teams. At the end of the week, we have a wrap-up, debriefing meeting wherein we talk about the true riches of life.

After spending a week in a different culture and seeing life from a totally different perspective, mission team participates' eyes are wide open to pondering the big picture of life.

This book has been written from material taken from this wrap-up meeting. The response of these mission teams to this information has been beyond inspirational. Hopefully, you'll find it life-changing as well.

May God receive all the glory for His role in this book. The true riches of life are His riches, the motivation to write this book was from Him, the strength to bring it to completion was from Him, and whatever blessing it brings will be because of Him.

Chapter 1

The Question of All Questions

Discovering the True Riches of Life

Can you think of a more important question than what the true riches of life are? Have you ever asked yourself this question? It's a deep subject and deserves some serious pondering and reflection. It shouldn't be answered lightly, as it's the question of all questions.

A number of years ago, a story was told of a reporter who interviewed Mohammad Ali, the famous boxer. During the interview at Ali's ranch, the reporter couldn't believe what he discovered. While in a large barn-like warehouse where Ali's trophies were, the reporter and Ali found themselves next to a large window. After some questioning, they took a short break. During this break, the reporter noticed Ali was staring out the window in a reflective, sober, far-away look. Then the reporter heard Ali mutter these words, "I had the world, and it didn't mean a thing."

As you probably know, Ali is considered the greatest boxer of all time. His fame and fortune reached the end of the earth. He had it all! Money, fame, respect, power, women, and so on. Yet in all this, he found emptiness and dissatisfaction.

The reporter continued with the interview, but then noticed a strange, white residue on all the trophies in Ali's warehouse. Upon closer inspection, the reporter discovered that it was pigeon droppings. How could it be? All these trophies that Ali had worked so hard to earn were now defaced, unappreciated, and forgotten.

Mohammad Ali had pursued what he thought were the true riches of life, but it ended in disillusionment. Ali had the world, and it didn't mean a thing.

Chapter 1: The Question of All Questions

Not All That Glitters Is Gold

Many people are like Mohammad Ali. They're pursuing the same riches he did. Like Ali experienced, most people's values and pursuits aren't bringing them what they hoped. Their search is leading them down a dead-end path of misery, disillusionment, and heartbreak. Instead of finding the pot of gold at the end of the rainbow, they're finding pain and emptiness.

It might be, though, that some people are happy in their pursuit of what they believe the true riches of life are. However, just because they're happy doesn't mean what they're seeking are true riches. If we're misguided, there will be consequences down the road in this life and in eternity as well.

How Can We Know What the True Riches of Life Are?

It might be that you've asked yourself the question regarding what the true riches of life are, but you've just taken for granted that what most people believe is right. After all, the majority couldn't be wrong, could they?

In order to discover and understand the true riches of life, we need to go to a source that is time-tested and authoritative. I believe this source is God, not what the majority of people believe. After all, He is the One who made us and knows us best. He is the One who created life and all that exists and knows what the true riches of life are.

Discovering the True Riches of Life

I'm moved by what God says in Isaiah 4:6–8:

All flesh [humanity] is grass, and all its beauty is like the flower of the field. The grass withers, the flower fades when the breath of the Lord blows on it; surely the people are grass. The grass withers, the flower fades, but the word of our God will stand forever.

God has revealed Himself and spoken to mankind through His Word, the Bible. Therefore, we can rest assured that it has the time-tested truth regarding what the true riches of life are.

Can We Trust the Bible?

You might ask, "Why is the Bible trustworthy and how can I be certain it contains the true riches of life?" That's a good question! Following are some brief ways we can know the Bible is from God and unlike any other writing known to humanity:

- *It contains prophecy:* There is no other writing that contains the wealth and detail of prophecy like the Bible. This is one of the key ways God confirms to us that He is the Author of the Bible because only He can know the future. It's true that some writings attempt to add their own prophecies, but they are very vague and unverifiable.

- *Jesus existed and performed countless miracles:* It is indisputable that Christ existed, performed a myriad of miracles, and changed the course of world history. Our calendar and holidays verify

Chapter 1: The Question of All Questions

this. Jesus claimed to be God in the flesh who came to be the Savior of the world and verified this by His life, teachings, miracles, and resurrection from the dead.

- ***Christ affirmed the Bible to be the very Word of God:*** Christ continually made statements concerning Scripture, such as *"It is written," "So that the Scripture might be fulfilled,"* and *"Have you not read?"* He also used it continuously in His ministry and teaching: *"And he said to them, 'O foolish ones, and slow of heart to believe all that the prophets have spoken! Was it not necessary that the Christ should suffer these things and enter into his glory?' And beginning with Moses and all the Prophets, he interpreted to them in all the Scriptures the things concerning himself"* (Luke 24:25-27).

- ***Christ claimed to be the very Word of God***: John 1:1 boldly states, *"In the beginning was the Word, and the Word was with God, and the Word was God."* Then John clarifies who the Word is: *"The **Word became flesh and dwelt among us**, and we have seen his glory, glory as of the only Son from the Father, full of grace and truth"* (John 1:14). Not only do we have the written Word of God that claims to be living, but this living Word also is a Person called Jesus Christ.

- ***The Bible claims to be inspired and contain the very words of God:*** 2 Timothy 3:16-17 states, *"All*

Scripture is breathed out by God and profitable for teaching, for reproof, for correction, and for training in righteousness, that the man of God may be competent, equipped for every good work." Also, 2 Peter 1:20-21 affirms, *"Knowing this first of all, that no prophecy of Scripture comes from someone's own interpretation. For no prophecy was ever produced by the will of man, but men spoke from God as they were carried along by the Holy Spirit."* Unlike any other writing known to mankind, Scripture claims to be the very words of God.

- **The Bible claims to be living:** Hebrews 4:12 asserts, *"For the word of God is living and active, sharper than any two-edged sword, piercing to the division of soul and of spirit, of joints and of marrow, and discerning the thoughts and intentions of the heart."* Scripture is living and active because God inhabits His Word and speaks through it. No other writing is like it.

- **The apostles affirmed the Bible as the very Word of God:** The apostles asserted that Scripture was inspired and used it continually. For example, Peter quoted large passages of Scripture in his sermon on the day of Pentecost, as found in Acts 2:14-42. The other apostles also used a heavy dose of Scripture in their ministries.

- **The New Testament writers affirmed the Bible as the very Word of God:** God fashioned the New Testament to rest upon the foundation of the Old Testament. Therefore, God inspired the human

Chapter 1: The Question of All Questions

writers of the New Testament to quote the Old Testament an amazing 855 times.[1] Many of these quotes were by Christ Himself, which gives further validation that Scripture is inspired and the very Word of God.

- *History supports the Bible as being the Word of God:* The Bible has been the most important writing in the history of humanity. From its inception until the present, it has been the most read, the most valued, the most copied, the most discussed, the most quoted, and the most sold piece of literature ever. It ranks far above all other writings.

- *The Bible claims to be eternal:* The Prophet Isaiah wrote, *"The grass withers, the flower fades, but the word of our God will stand forever"* (Isa. 40:8). The Apostle Peter penned, *"But the word of the Lord remains forever. And this word is the good news that was preached to you"* (1 Pet. 1:25). Moreover, Christ proclaimed, *"Heaven and earth will pass away, but my words will not pass away"* (Matt. 24:35).

- *Countless people claim that Jesus Christ has changed their lives:* Millions and millions of people claim that Jesus Christ has transformed their lives and have been willing to die for Him.

- *The Bible contains supernatural teachings:* The nature of the teachings in the Bible are supernatural

---

[1] Blue Letter Bible, BlueLetterBible.org, *Study Resources: Charts and Quotes*, www.blueletterbible.org/study/pnt/pnt08.cfm, Accessed 10/14/2016.

and good. They are far above human thinking and promote, in most cases, exactly the opposite of what mankind would propose.

The Perspective of This Book

Because I believe the Bible is the Word of God, I will be using its truths to communicate what the true riches of life are. I have a deep passion for the Bible and have invested many years in theological training in order to better understand it. As a result, my desire is to faithfully handle Scripture and let God speak for Himself.

Thus, this book contains a great deal of Scripture, some of which you might have read before. However, I want to encourage you to slow down, be reflective, and allow God to speak to you afresh. God's Word is living, so no matter how many times we've read a verse, if we'll ponder and allow it to sink in, God will bring new insights and change to our lives.

A Lot Is at Stake

Discovering what the true riches of life are is the most important question we could pursue. A lot is riding on the answer. Not only does it affect our present life, but our eternity as well. Therefore, it's paramount we get it right. We can't afford to be wrong in this vital area as it will greatly affect this life and the one to come.

Chapter 2

What Are You Seeking in Life?

Discovering the True Riches of Life

Everyone is searching for something in life whether they realize it or not. What are you searching for? Some are searching for recognition, popularity, social status, happiness, love, wealth, ease of life, peace, and so on. Everyone is subconsciously in a pursuit for what they believe will bring them meaning and fulfillment.

A Myriad of Options at Our Disposal

In our age, we have a record amount of choices facing us. Gone are the days when life was simpler, less tangled, and had fewer details and problems. We're now faced with countless impulses and stimuli from things like sports, social media, texting, phone calls, emails, Internet, TV, magazines, billboards, friends, work, entertainment, and on and on.

Television alone has revolutionized the Western world in staggering ways. Here are recent statistics on how much the average person in the U.S. watches TV:[2]

- Average time spent watching television per day ~ 5 hours and 11 minutes
- Years the average person will have spent watching TV in their lifetime ~ 9 years
- Percentage of U.S. homes with three or more TV sets ~ 65%
- Number of minutes per week the average child watches TV ~ 1,480 (24.66 hours)
- Percentage of Americans that regularly watch TV

---

[2] Statistic Brain Research Institute, *Television Watching Statistics*, 2015, www.statisticbrain.com/television-watching-statistics, Accessed 08/07/2016.

Chapter 2: What Are You Seeking in Life?

while eating dinner ~ 67%
- Hours per year the average American youth watches TV ~ 1,200 (50 days)
- Number of violent acts seen on TV by age 18 ~ 150,000
- Number of 30 second TV commercials seen in a year by an average child ~ 16,000

In addition to TV, we have countless other options in our lives. Many of these things are not wrong in and of themselves; it's just that we allow them into our lives in an excessive amount so that they choke out the true riches of life. They distract us from storing up riches in heaven and pursuing what's most important.

Are You a Product of Your Culture?

In addition to the previously mentioned things that most people are seeking in life, there are other factors contributing to what we believe the true riches of life are.

As mentioned, I'm a long-term missionary in Mexico. Our ministry receives many short-term mission teams throughout the year, and we always end the week with a debriefing time. During this time, we talk about the different values and customs between the cultures of the U.S./Canada and Mexico. Our goal is to help these short-term mission teams assimilate all they've experienced in Mexico back into their own culture in a healthy, biblical way. The following are some interesting differences between the values between the U.S./Canada and other cultures:

- The U.S. and Canada place a high value on happiness, while other cultures of the world place a high value on peace and tranquility. A "Happiness Culture" views happiness as their highest goal in life. A "Peace Culture" views peace and tranquility as their highest goal in life.

- The U.S. and Canada place a high value on "doing," wherein other cultures place a high value on "being." A "Doing Culture" measures spirituality and worth more by doing. A "Being Culture" measures spirituality and worth more by being (attitudes).

- The U.S. and Canada are "Time-Oriented" cultures while other cultures are "Event Oriented." A "Time-Oriented" culture focuses on time; they tend to be punctual, efficient and quick. Things start on time and end on time. An "Event-Oriented" culture focuses more on the moment at hand, and less on time and the future.

- The U.S. and Canada are dominantly "Independent-Oriented" cultures while many other cultures are "Interdependent-Oriented." An "Independent-Oriented" culture doesn't rely much on one another to get by in life because they've grown up believing they don't need their parents, grandparents, and extended family very much.

  Also, most "Independent-Oriented" cultures are

Chapter 2: What Are You Seeking in Life?

wealthy and have about everything they need. They have their own homes, cars, electronic devices, tools, skills, knowledge, and so on. This causes them to be independent instead of interdependent.

An "Interdependent-Oriented" culture has grown up closely intertwined with family. Family is very important and viewed as essential. Also, interdependent cultures generally aren't as wealthy, and therefore, family and relationships are viewed as more important. In an interdependent culture, people need one another to get by in life. Everyone helps each other out, and together they go through life as a community.

Whether we fully understand it or not, we're affected by the culture in which we live. Therefore, it's easy for us to adopt our culture's values without even realizing it. Unless we stop and really analyze our values in life, we'll drift along with our culture. In so doing, we could be adopting our culture's standards instead of what God says are the true riches of life.

Happiness and Entertainment: The Gods of the 21st Century

The gods of our day are happiness and entertainment, and most people are lost in the pursuit of them. It's almost become standard procedure today that everything we do must first be run through the filter of pleasure and convenience. If it's not fun, thrilling, and exciting, we want no part of it.

Some people even think it's okay to disobey certain commands of Scripture if it makes a person happy. They view happiness as supreme. They believe God wants us to be happy, so even if our lifestyles don't quite harmonize with Scripture, it's okay. They've bought into our culture's view that God's primary goal for us is happiness. This should be of no surprise as the message many pastors preach today is a continual focus on the blessings of God and how He wants us to be happy.

Today, the scales are so tilted toward happiness that many believe it's their right. They fail to understand that God hasn't called us to be happy and entertained, but devoted and fruitful. God wants to replace our pursuit of happiness and pleasure with genuine joy and purpose. He wants us to lose our lives for Him so we can find the true riches of life.

Entertainment and the Last Days

One of our greatest enemies in the pursuit of the true riches of life is entertainment. Life for many people is primarily about fun, thrill, and having a good time. Essential character that helps us attain the true riches of life such as self-discipline, responsibility, hard work, patience, endurance, suffering, faithfulness, and service are lacking in the lives of many. We're living in the last days as described in 2 Timothy 3:1–5:

> *But understand this, that in the last days there will come times of difficulty. For people will be **lovers of***

Chapter 2: What Are You Seeking in Life?

*self, **lovers of money**, proud, arrogant, abusive, disobedient to their parents, ungrateful, unholy, heartless, unappeasable, slanderous, without self-control, brutal, not loving good, treacherous, reckless, swollen with conceit, **lovers of pleasure rather than lovers of God**, having the appearance of godliness, but denying its power. Avoid such people.*

This pretty well sums up our culture today, and unfortunately, it's affecting the lives of most people. Most are "lovers of pleasure rather than lovers of God" and are not very interested in seeking the true riches of life.

Boredom Is at an All-Time High

Despite all our busyness and activity, boredom is off the charts. Why is this so? Why do children, students, and adults feel so unsatisfied today? If busyness and pleasure bring happiness, why is boredom plaguing many today? It's because God made us to serve Him and not ourselves. We only find meaning and value in the true riches of life, and until we understand this, we can gain the whole world and all its pleasures, but still be empty.

What Are Your Priorities?

Never in the history of any civilization have there been so many stimuli and activities available. How is this affecting our pursuit of the true riches of life? I believe it's reeking catastrophic consequences!

Discovering the True Riches of Life

My mother made a wise statement about priorities many years ago, saying, "We always have time for what's important to us." I believe she's right! It's not that we don't have time; it's that our priorities are out of line. We're so caught up in the distractions of our current age that we don't take time for Christ and the true riches of life.

Chapter 3

True Riches #1
Being Right with God

Discovering the True Riches of Life

There is no greater joy, purpose, peace, satisfaction, or pleasure that can compare with being right with God. Deep within us God has placed the need for us to be right with Him, and when we're not, everything is messed up, and we're out of kilter.

Why Is It Important to Be Right with God?

Only a small percentage of people think it's important to be right with God. Most will live their lives with no regard to God or what He thinks. If most people don't think it's important to be right with God, should you? After all, wouldn't the majority be right? Sadly, according to Scripture, the majority of the time the majority of people are wrong. Let's look at why it's so imperative that we be right with God.

It's Important to Be Right with God Because He Is Everything

"The heavens declare the glory of God; and the firmament shows his handiwork" (Ps. 19:1 NKJV).

In order to move around in God's universe, we need a huge ruler. Let's use the speed of light as our ruler. Light travels at the speed of 186,000 miles per second. That's over 11 million miles an hour. Light can circle our globe 7.5 times per second. That's astounding! Our modern commercial airplanes travel at around 550 miles per hour. It would take an airplane 14 days to travel what light can do in a second. It takes

Chapter 3: Being Right with God

light about 1.3 seconds to travel from the moon to the earth. It would take an airplane about 18 days to do the same. It takes light about 8.5 minutes to travel from the sun to the earth; it would take an airplane around 20 years to do the same. It takes light around 5.5 hours to travel from the sun to Pluto, which is currently the farthest planet (dwarf planet) away in our solar system. It would take an airplane 774 years to do the same. So, for light to cross our solar system, it would take about 11 hours. It would take an airplane 1,548 years.

Our Solar System

Our solar system resides in the Milky Way Galaxy in the perfect location for life to exist. If it were any closer or farther away, life couldn't survive. Our galaxy boasts of somewhere between 100 and 400 billion stars. It takes light approximately 100,000 light years to cross it. It's a massive galaxy, but tiny in comparison to others. For example, a recently discovered galaxy called 1C 1101 is about 6 million light-years in diameter and has a mass of about 100 trillion stars. That's unbelievable!

Milky Way Galaxy

Now let's consider something even more staggering! Our galaxy is just one among countless other galaxies in our universe. Do you have any idea how many galaxies there are in our universe? Latest estimates say that there are between 100 and 500 billion galaxies discovered to date. This number is far less than what there really is because the universe is beyond scientist's ability to discover. It virtually has no end.

That's an incomprehensible number of galaxies! In order to better understand this number for our finite minds, it would be like holding a sharp pencil out at arm's length and, from our eye's viewpoint, there would be over a thousand galaxies that would fit behind the tip of that pencil.

But what's even more amazing is that God says He holds all the galaxies in the universe in the palm of His hand: *"Who has measured the waters in the hollow of his hand, or with the breadth of his hand marked off the heavens? Who has held the dust of the earth in a basket, or weighed the mountains on the scales and the hills in a balance?"* (Isa. 40:12 NIV).

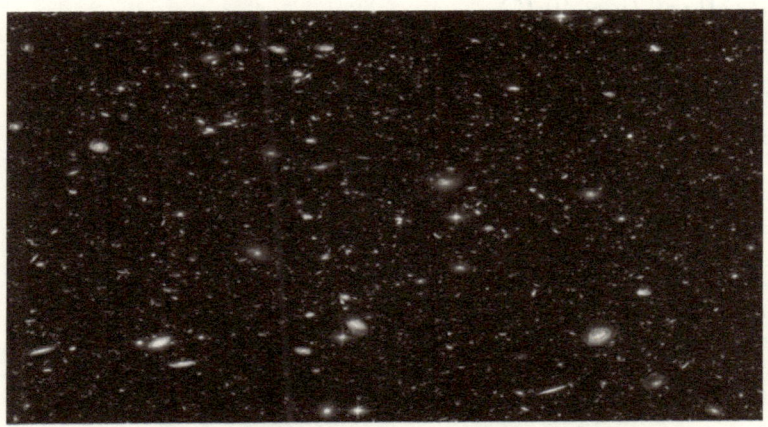

Part of Our Universe (what you see are all galaxies)

God is much bigger than the heavens. Therefore, He can hold them in the palm of His hand. God is what we call, theologically, transcendent. That means He is bigger than, outside of, and transcends the universe. He is the one who made it, so He is obviously much greater and bigger than it.

For God to even enter the universe is like crawling into a tiny sized dog house. He simply can't fit. King Solomon acknowledged this truth by stating, *"But will God indeed dwell with man on the earth? Behold, heaven, and the highest heaven cannot contain you, how much less this house that I have built!"* (2 Chron. 6:18).

The great prophet, Isaiah, proclaimed, *"Do you not*

know? Do you not hear? Has it not been told you from the beginning? Have you not understood from the foundations of the earth? It is he who sits above the circle of the earth, and its inhabitants are like grasshoppers; who stretches out the heavens like a curtain, and spreads them like a tent to dwell in" (Isa. 40:12).

God is also so big that He calls each star by name: *"To whom then will you compare me, that I should be like him? Says the Holy One. Lift up your eyes on high and see: who created these? He who brings out their host by number, calling them all by name; by the greatness of his might and because he is strong in power, not one is missing"* (Isa. 40:25-26).

God never grows weary, and His omnipotence (infinite power) has no bounds: *"Have you not known? Have you not heard? The Lord is the everlasting God, the Creator of the ends of the earth. He does not faint or grow weary; his understanding is unsearchable. He gives power to the faint, and to him who has no might he increases strength"* (Isa. 40:28-29).

Why is it important to be right with God? For starters, He is the Creator of everything, gives life to everything, sustains everything, and all things exist by Him and for Him. The very next breath we breathe is due to His grace and power, and no life would exist outside of Him. In short, He is everything!

He feeds all the animals, causes all things to grow, and keeps the universe running in perfect harmony and balance:

Chapter 3: Being Right with God

You make springs gush forth in the valleys; they flow between the hills; they give drink to every beast of the field; the wild donkeys quench their thirst. Beside them the birds of the heavens dwell; they sing among the branches. From your lofty abode you water the mountains; the earth is satisfied with the fruit of your work. You cause the grass to grow for the livestock and plants for man to cultivate, that he may bring forth food from the earth and wine to gladden the heart of man, oil to make his face shine and bread to strengthen man's heart" (Ps. 104:10–15).

It's Important to Be Right with God Because He Is Everywhere

Not only is God everything, but He's also everywhere. Theologically, we call this being omnipresent. However, God is everywhere in a different sense than what you and I probably think.

I can understand that God is big, but He also has a lot to do and a lot of places to be. So, in my finite mind, I tend to think that He divides Himself up among every place and every person and we all might get a small percentage of Him. The truth of the matter, though, is that He is 100% everywhere 100% of the time. That's an amazing truth! You and I each have 100% of God's attention 100% of the time. This is why David could say, *"How precious to me are your thoughts, O God! How vast is the sum of them! If I would count them, they are more than the sand. I awake, and I am still with you"* (Ps. 139:17–18).

God is always thinking about us and never takes His mind off us. His thoughts toward each one of us are more than the sand on all the seashores (which is stressing and infinite amount).

Sometimes we might feel like God is far away and doesn't hear us. However, that's just not the truth. Regardless of how we might feel, it doesn't change reality. Scripture verifies this by the following statement of David: *"O Lord, you have searched me and known me! You know when I sit down and when I rise up; you discern my thoughts from afar. You search out my path and my lying down and are acquainted with all my ways. Even before a word is on my tongue, behold, O Lord, you know it altogether"* (Ps. 139:1-4).

God searches our hearts, knows us intimately, and is acquainted with all our movements. He knows when we sit down and stand up. He knows our thoughts from afar. He even knows what we're going to say before we speak. We have a God who is always thinking of us and loves us deeply.

In addition, we might feel like in order for God to hear our prayers we should get as many people to pray for us as we can. This, we think, will kind of make a noise in the universe and God will better hear us. It's great to ask others to pray for us, and the more, the merrier. However, just because we have a lot of people praying for us doesn't affect whether God hears us. God hears us no matter what: *"For the eyes of the Lord are on the righteous, and his ears are open to their prayer.*

Chapter 3: Being Right with God

But the face of the Lord is against those who do evil" (1 Pet. 3:12).

It's Important to Be Right with God Because He Is All-Powerful

Not only is God everything and everywhere, but He is also all-powerful. We call this being omnipotent. There is no limit to God's power and abilities.

We see one of God's greatest displays of power in the creation of the heavens and earth: *"It is he who made the earth by his power, who established the world by his wisdom, and by his understanding stretched out the heavens"* (Jer. 10:12). And again, *"Thus says the Lord, your Redeemer, who formed you from the womb: 'I am the Lord, who made all things, who alone stretched out the heavens, who spread out the earth by myself"* (Isa. 44:24).

God never grows weary or tired, and His strength is unending and timeless: *"Have you not known? Have you not heard? The Lord is the everlasting God, the Creator of the ends of the earth. He does not faint or grow weary; his understanding is unsearchable"* (Isa. 40:28).

It's Important to Be Right with God Because He Is Eternal

Not only is God everything, everywhere, and all-powerful, but He is also eternal. He has neither beginning nor end of days. He is timeless and everlasting.

We can count to a hundred in about a minute, we can count to a thousand in about 10 minutes, and we can count to a million in about three weeks. If you want to count to a billion, however, you'll need to start early in life because it's going to take you 77 years. And counting to a trillion would take 77,000 years, so it's impossible in a single lifetime.

God is eternal, has always existed, and will always exist: *"Before the mountains were brought forth, or ever you had formed the earth and the world, from everlasting to everlasting you are God"* (Ps. 90:2).

Nebuchadnezzar also learned this truth after enduring God's judgment for a time. He said, *"At the end of the days I, Nebuchadnezzar, lifted my eyes to heaven, and my reason returned to me, and I blessed the Most High, and praised and honored him who lives forever, for his dominion is an everlasting dominion, and his kingdom endures from generation to generation"* (Dan. 4:34).

God has also made us eternal beings as well. Solomon wrote, *"He has made everything beautiful in its time. Also, he has put **eternity into man's heart**, yet so that he cannot find out what God has done from the beginning to the end"* (Eccl. 3:11).

Because we are eternal beings, we will all spend eternity in one of two places; heaven or hell. Christ affirmed this when He spoke about the time He will judge and separate the righteous from the unrighteous: *"And these will go away into eternal punishment, but the righteous into eternal life"* (Matt. 25:46).

Chapter 3: Being Right with God

Consequences for Not Being Right with God

There are great rewards for being right with God and great consequences for not being right with Him. The following is a sobering passage that speaks about the consequences of not being right with God:

> *Then I saw a great white throne and him who was seated on it. From his presence earth and sky fled away, and no place was found for them. And I saw the dead, great and small, standing before the throne, and books were opened. Then another book was opened, which is the book of life. And the dead were judged by what was written in the books, according to what they had done. And the sea gave up the dead who were in it, Death and Hades [the grave] gave up the dead who were in them, and they were judged, each one of them, according to what they had done. Then Death and Hades were thrown into the **lake of fire**. This is the second death, the **lake of fire**. And if anyone's name was not found written in the book of life, he was thrown into the **lake of fire*** (Rev. 20:11–15).

This passage speaks of the time when each person who has not trusted in Christ for salvation will be judged. It's commonly known as "The Great White Throne Judgment." It will be a horrifying time as multitudes, who cared less about God while they were living, now embrace the judgment for their carefree living and rejection of God.

It should be noted that God loves everyone and Christ died on the Cross to be the payment for our sins. However, when people knowingly reject this truth, they are choosing to incur God's eternal judgment upon themselves.

Heaven and Earth Won't Stand God's Presence

At the Great White Throne Judgment, it says, *"From his presence earth and sky fled away, and no place was found for them"* (Rev. 20:11). This indicates that not even the heavens and earth will be able to stand God's presence at this judgment. In a sense, God is also judging His creation that has been corrupted by mankind's sin and rebellion: *"Behold, God puts no trust in his holy ones, and the heavens are not pure in his sight; how much less one who is abominable and corrupt, a man who drinks injustice like water!"* (Job 15:15–16).

Not only will God judge non-Christians, but the heavens and earth as well. He will destroy them and then create new heavens and a new earth: *"Lift up your eyes to the heavens, and look at the earth beneath; for the heavens vanish like smoke, the earth will wear out like a garment, and they who dwell in it will die in like manner; but my salvation will be forever, and my righteousness will never be dismayed"* (Isa. 51:6). Again, Scripture declares, *"But according to his promise we are waiting for new heavens and a new earth in which righteousness dwells"* (2 Pet. 3:13).

Chapter 3: Being Right with God

Don't Ignore God's Voice

Being right with God is the most important duty for each person. God loves us, seeks us, and desires to give us salvation and life. However, for those who reject this priceless gift, there awaits the sober reality of spending eternity separated from God in hell. Therefore, now is the time to get right with God before it's too late. We should not refuse and neglect God's voice:

> *See that you do not refuse him who is speaking. For if they did not escape when they refused him who warned them on earth, much less will we escape if we reject him who warns from heaven. At that time his voice shook the earth, but now he has promised, "Yet once more I will shake not only the earth but also the heavens." This phrase, "Yet once more," indicates the removal of things that are shaken — that is, things that have been made — in order that the things that cannot be shaken may remain* (Heb. 12:25-27).

At this judgment time, God says, *"Therefore I will make the heavens tremble, and the earth will be shaken out of its place, at the wrath of the Lord of hosts in the day of his fierce anger"* (Isa. 13:13).

God is a God of love, but He is also a God of justice, and He will not let sin and rebellion go unpunished. He will not let the rebellious and sinful person into His heaven. For He says, *"Be assured, an evil person will not go unpunished, but the offspring of the righteous will be delivered"* (Prov. 11:21). Again, God says:

Or do you not know that the unrighteous will not inherit the kingdom of God? Do not be deceived: neither the sexually immoral, nor idolaters, nor adulterers, nor men who practice homosexuality, nor thieves, nor the greedy, nor drunkards, nor revilers, nor swindlers will inherit the kingdom of God. (1 Cor. 6:9–10).

My Humble Question for the Non-Christian

This is the humble question I have for all my non-Christian friends, and I ask it with all due respect: "If on Judgment Day the heavens and earth won't be able to stand the presence of God, what makes you think you will? You, a fragile creature whose next breath is only possible because of God's grace, do you think you are more powerful than the heavens and earth and will withstand God's judgment upon you?"

We live in a day when we focus heavily upon God's love. We speak of His grace, forgiveness, kindness, and so on. However, biblically speaking, God is also a just God who will punish those who choose to reject Him their whole life. We tend to presume upon God's love and think everyone will go to heaven when they die. After all, when's the last time you went to a funeral of a non-Christian and heard the preacher say the deceased was now in hell? We gloss over these realities and live as if hell doesn't exist and no one is going there.

Moreover, for those who reject God and want nothing to do with Him while they are on earth, why would they want to spend eternity in heaven with Him anyway? They have already demonstrated that they want nothing to do with God.

In essence, being in hell is being separated from God and all that is good. So, for the person who wants nothing to do with God, they are choosing hell. It is their choice, not God's.

The Books Are Opened, and People Are Judged

*"And I saw the dead, great and small, standing before the throne, **and books were opened**. Then another book was opened, which is the book of life. And the dead were judged by what was written in the books, according to what they had done. And the sea gave up the dead who were in it, Death and Hades [the grave] gave up the dead who were in them, and they were judged, each one of them, according to what they had done. Then Death and Hades were thrown into the lake of fire. This is the second death, the lake of fire. **And if anyone's name was not found written in the book of life, he was thrown into the lake of fire**"* (Rev. 20:12–15).

For those whose names are not written in the Book of Life, God is keeping track of every deed they are doing and will hold them accountable.

Those whose names are written in the Book of Life will not be judged at the Great White Throne because they have received Christ as their Savior and their sins have been paid for by Christ's sacrifice on the Cross.

However, for the non-Christian, they will pay for their sins and rebellion to God in hell. You see, God's justice demands that sin and rebellion be paid for.

Either we can choose to let Christ pay for them, or we can pay for them on our own. If we choose Christ, then He pays for our sins and gives us eternal life in heaven. If we reject Christ, then we are choosing to pay for our own sins for which the penalty is eternity in hell.

Non-Christians Are Cast into the Lake of Fire

*"Then Death and Hades were thrown into the **lake of fire**. This is the second death, the **lake of fire**. And if anyone's name was not found written in the book of life, he was thrown into the **lake of fire**"* (Rev. 20:14-15).

Hell is not a popular topic today, but that doesn't change the fact of its reality. It's like the existence of gravity, it doesn't matter what people might believe or say about its existence, gravity exists. Virtually all people and every religion believe in heaven. However, the same verses in the Bible that speak about the reality of heaven also speak about the reality of hell. Lovingly said, we can't just choose what we want and disregard what we don't like. We are not God who gets to decide what truth is. Our responsibility is to believe the truth and proclaim its realities.

Christ was the leading figure who talked about hell in the Bible. In fact, He spoke more about hell and the judgments of God than about heaven. He described hell as:

- A fiery lake of burning sulfur that is unquenchable and never goes out (Matt. 25:46; Mark 9:43-44; Rev. 21:8).

Chapter 3: Being Right with God

- Everlasting destruction away from the presence of the Lord (2 Thess. 1:9).
- Where people will gnash their teeth in pain (Matt. 13:50).
- Where the devil and the demons suffer (Matt. 25:41).
- A gloomy dungeon (2 Pet. 2:4).
- Where the worm never dies (Mark 9:48).
- A fiery furnace (Matt. 13:42).
- Where people will be salted with fire (Mark 9:49).
- A place of weeping (Matt. 13:50).
- A place of utter darkness (Jude 1:13).
- A place of fiery flames (Luke 16:24).
- A place of torment (Luke 16:28).

According to Christ, hell is a real place, and many will choose to go there because of their rejection of Christ. They'll choose materialism, pleasure, and the pride of life over the salvation of their souls and the eternal riches of Christ.

How to Become Right with God for the Non-Christian

For the non-Christian, being right with God involves salvation. It's impossible to be right with God without being saved. This is where it all begins.

There's nothing more important to God than that we be right with Him. As our Creator, He loves us more than we can imagine and desires a relationship with us. He wants to bless us, give us life, grant us His Spirit, impart eternal life to us, restore broken relationships, share with us His principles for how to live, and offer us meaning and purpose in life.

When I was 18 years old, I read a book by Billy Graham called *How to Be Born Again*. This book walked me through the steps of what my problem was and how God wanted to help me. After I read it, I literally begged God with tear-filled eyes to come into my life and change me. He more than answered my prayer and I can't begin to share everything God has done in my life and how He has transformed me.

The following are the simple, yet life transforming steps that I took many years ago, and that those of you who are not born-again can take to become saved and have your names written in the Book of Life:

Step 1: God loves us and desires that we would spend eternity in heaven with Him.

John 3:16: *"For God so loved the world, that he gave his only Son, that whoever believes in him should not perish but have eternal life."*

Step 2: Our sin and rejection of God separate us from Him.

Genesis 2:15-17: *"The Lord God took the man and put him in the Garden of Eden to work it and keep it. And the Lord God commanded the man, saying, 'You may surely eat of every tree of the garden, but of the tree of the knowledge of*

Chapter 3: Being Right with God

good and evil you shall not eat, for in the day that you eat of it you shall surely die.'"

<u>Isaiah 59:2</u>: *"But your iniquities have made a separation between you and your God, and your sins have hidden his face from you so that he does not hear."*

<u>Romans 3:23</u>: *"For all have sinned and fall short of the glory of God."*

Summary of steps 1 and 2: We have lost our relationship with God our Creator and, as a result, have a sinful heart. We do not desire to please God and are selfish and sinful. Our greatest sin is that of not having a relationship with God and loving Him as our Father and Creator. If the greatest command in the Bible is to love the Lord our God with all our heart, soul, mind, and strength, then our greatest sin is not to love and have a relationship with Him. This is our primary sin (Matt. 7:21-23).

Step 3: The price for practicing sin and rejecting God is eternity in hell.

<u>Romans 6:23</u>: *"For the wages of sin is death, but the free gift of God is eternal life in Christ Jesus our Lord."*

<u>Matthew 13:49-50</u>: *"So it will be at the end of the age. The angels will come out and separate the evil from the righteous and throw them into the fiery furnace. In that place there will be weeping and gnashing of teeth."*

<u>Revelation 21:8</u>: *"But as for the cowardly, the faithless, the detestable, as for murderers, the sexually immoral,*

sorcerers, idolaters, and all liars, their portion will be in the lake that burns with fire and sulfur, which is the second death."

Step 4: God's remedy for our sin is abundant, eternal life through Christ's death on the Cross and resurrection from the dead.

Isaiah 53:5: *"But he was pierced for our transgressions; he was crushed for our iniquities; upon him was the chastisement that brought us peace, and with his wounds we are healed."*

Romans 5:8: *"But God shows his love for us in that while we were still sinners, Christ died for us."*

Romans 6:23: *"For the wages of sin is death, but the free gift of God is eternal life in Christ Jesus our Lord."*

Ephesians 2:8-9: *"For by grace you have been saved through faith. And this is not your own doing; it is the gift of God, not a result of works, so that no one may boast."*

Step 5: Would you like to receive Christ and His gift of eternal life?

John 1:12: *"But to all who did receive him, who believed in his name, he gave the right to become children of God."*

John 3:36: *"Whoever believes in the Son has eternal life; whoever does not obey the Son shall not see life, but the wrath of God remains on him."*

Acts 4:12: *"And there is salvation in no one else, for there is no other name under heaven given among men by which we must be saved."*

Step 6: How to receive Christ as Lord and Savior.

1. Admit that you are a sinner in need of a Savior.
2. Believe that Christ died on the Cross to pay for your sins and rose from the dead to give you eternal life.
3. Believe that without Christ's payment for your sins you deserve hell.
4. Repent and confess that you are a sinner, asking for God's forgiveness and grace.
5. Pray to receive Christ and His gift of salvation.
6. Give your heart and will to Christ.

Being Right with God for the Christian

For the born-again believer, being right with God involves being in good standing with Him. It doesn't refer to perfection, but to a Christian who has no unconfessed sin in their life, is not practicing any unbiblical activities, is growing in Christ as an obedient disciple, is serious about their relationship with God, and has no broken relationships with others wherein they haven't asked forgiveness for any ways they are at fault.

Being Right with God Means Having a Clear Conscience

Being right with God can be summarized as having a clear conscience before God and others.

This was a repeated theme in the life of the Apostle Paul. When on trial for his faith in Christ, before Felix in Caesarea, he stated:

> *But this I confess to you, that according to the Way, which they call a sect, I worship the God of our fathers, believing everything laid down by the Law and written in the Prophets, having a hope in God, which these men themselves accept, that there will be a resurrection of both the just and the unjust. So I always* **take pains to have a clear conscience** *toward both God and man* (Acts 24:14-16).

Because Paul believed there would be a resurrection of the dead for both the just and unjust, he took great pains to have a clear conscience before God and man.

Hopefully, we as Christians are taking "great pains" to be right with God and others as well. However, for many Christians, this is not the case. They are not truly at peace with God and have broken relationships with others they haven't attempted to fix by asking forgiveness for their part in the matter.

Close to the end of Paul's life, when writing to Timothy, he again shared his lifelong commitment to having a clear conscience, *"I thank God whom I serve, as did my ancestors,* **with a clear conscience***, as I remember you constantly in my prayers night and day"* (2 Tim. 1:3).

Paul also referred to the importance of a clear conscience when giving the requirements for church leaders. He affirms, *"They must hold the mystery of the faith with a* **clear conscience***"* (1 Tim. 3:9). Having a clear conscience before God and others is so important that it was included as a requirement for any leadership role in the church.

The writer of Hebrews also speaks of the value of a clear conscience. He says, *"Pray for us, for we are sure that we have a **clear conscience**, desiring to act honorably in all things"* (Heb. 13:18).

Once again, being right with God doesn't mean we are perfect, but that we are in a right relationship with God and others. This means we are to be in close, obedient fellowship with God and have done all in our power to be at peace with others.

What Keeps Us from Being Right with God?

Life can be pretty simple at times. Basically, we have two options in every life-moment. We can do what we want or what God wants. It's a matter of who is lord or the master in our lives. Christ says we can't serve two masters. The biggest factor that keeps both the Christian and non-Christian from being right with God is our own wills. The non-Christian doesn't want to submit to God and let Him be the boss of their lives. The Christian has submitted to God but struggles to remain under submission and choose God's will over theirs as they live their Christian life.

Christ spoke clearly about this struggle and likened it to "saving" your life and "losing" it. To "save" your life is to remain the boss of it and do what you want to do. It's about control. Will you or God be in control? To "lose" your life means we let God be in control, and we do His will.

Saving Your Life and Losing It

Christ said, *"For whoever desires to save his life will lose it, but whoever loses his life for My sake and the gospel's will save it. For what will it profit a man if he **gains the whole world, and loses his own soul?** Or what will a man give in exchange for his soul?"* (Mark 8:36–37, NKJV).

What does it profit to gain the whole world and lose your soul? This statement by Christ is a "no-brainer" question and a simple one to answer. It was a question posed by Christ to show the stupidity of even asking such a ridiculous question.

But to make matters worse, Christ showed the absurdity of our rationale in that, while no sane person would be willing to lose their soul at the expense of gaining the whole world, they are willing to lose it for the hope of gaining just a fraction of it. How unbelievable! Who would be willing to lose their soul for just gaining a little bit of the "good life"? Of course, no one would, right? That's the point of the question. Who in their right mind would choose to lose their soul at the expense of a few fleeting years of pleasure? No one, right? Wrong! That's exactly what most do.

Tragically, many surgeons, scientists, professionals, adults, and students can't do simple math. With all their brilliance, they can't even do a simple math equation that a 5-year-old can do. They value a few fleeting years of pleasure above all the eternal glories of heaven. Humbly said, that's the height of stupidity and foolishness. It's completely off the radar, incomprehensible, ridiculous, absurd, and ludicrous! Yet, it's what many choose in this life. What a tragedy!

Gaining the World and Christians Today

What about us Christians? While we recognize that gaining the world isn't worth losing our soul in hell, we do, however, by our actions, seem to believe that gaining the world is worth losing our eternal rewards in heaven.

Many Christians are caught up in materialism, pleasure, and prestige, and are sacrificing their eternal rewards on the altar for a few vanishing years of gratification. They are blind to the true riches of life, and instead, are gaining the world but losing their eternal rewards in the process. How foolish! God warns of this deadly trap in John 2:15-17:

> *Do not love the world or the things in the world. If anyone loves the world, the love of the Father is not in him. For all that is in the world – **the desires of the flesh and the desires of the eyes and pride of life** – is not from the Father but is from the world. And the world is passing away along with its desires, but whoever does the will of God abides forever.*

What hinders many Christians from seeking the true riches of life as their highest priority? God says it's the desires of the flesh (pleasure), the desires of the eyes (materialism), and the pride of life (prestige) — all of which are enemies of the true riches of life. They are choosing the pleasures of the world that are passing away and neglecting the eternal riches and rewards of heaven.

What Is the Purpose of Life?

The book of Ecclesiastes deals with the purpose of our existence. It answers the big question of life. God gave Solomon (the author of Ecclesiastes) extreme wisdom, wealth, power, and time to pursue what brings us meaning and purpose in life. With these resources at his disposal, he tested every major way we seek meaning and purpose to see if they answered the big question of life.

He sought wisdom and knowledge but didn't find the answer there. He had 300 wives and 700 concubines (a woman who is primarily a sexual mistress). However, he didn't find the answer in sex and human love. He was so wealthy that it was staggering (the wealthiest person on earth at that time), but he didn't find the answer in wealth. He was the most powerful man on earth, but didn't find the answer in power and prestige either. He sought meaning in work and accomplishment, and found it to be worthwhile, but not the answer he was looking for.

After it was all said and done, Solomon gave the summation of our purpose in life at the end of the book of Ecclesiastes. He said, *"The end of the matter; all has been heard.* **Fear God and keep his commandments, for this is the whole duty of man"** (Eccl. 12:13).

Chapter 3: Being Right with God

If we're honest, most of us are seeking one or more of the areas where Solomon looked for meaning and purpose in life. It's not that any area is wrong in and of itself, but it's not going to bring meaning and purpose if we neglect being right with God.

God positioned Solomon to be able to answer the purpose of life from a unique viewpoint. He was able to seek out each area by experiencing it to the max. Whether it be wisdom, knowledge, sex, human love, power, prestige, wealth, work, and so on, he exhausted each area to the fullest.

Sometimes we think if we can just get a little bit more in each area where Solomon looked for meaning and purpose, then we'll be satisfied. However, it's just not the truth. We could never attain the level Solomon acquired, so the answer is not there.

The whole duty of mankind is to be right with God. As Solomon stated, *"The end of the matter; all has been heard.* **Fear God and keep his commandments, for this is the whole duty of man"** (Eccl. 12:13).

Chapter 4

True Riches #2

Our Works and Service for Christ

Discovering the True Riches of Life

*"Do not lay up for yourselves treasures on earth, where moth and rust destroy and where thieves break in and steal, **but lay up for yourselves treasures in heaven**, where neither moth nor rust destroys and where thieves do not break in and steal. For where your treasure is, there your heart will be also"* (Matt. 6:19–21).

Where is your heart? What are you living for? Where is your treasure? What's more important to you, this life or heaven? Laying up treasures on earth is a short-sighted focus to life. Laying up treasures in heaven is a long-term focus. Christ emphasizes that in order to lay up treasures in heaven we need to place our heart there first.

God has given abundant revelation about heavenly rewards in Scripture. Running throughout its pages are rich illustrations and ample verses regarding this doctrine. In fact, it's a foundational theme of Scripture and one affiliated with the justice of God. It's only right that we are rewarded based on our actions and choices in this present life. Scripture teaches that according to how we live this life, we will be rewarded or punished in the next.

The Theme of Rewards in Scripture

The word "reward" or its variant is mentioned around 82 times in the Bible. The following are just a few verses that speak about the reality of rewards:

Chapter 4: Our Works and Service for Christ

- ***Isaiah 40:10:*** *"Behold, the Lord God comes with might, and his arm rules for him; behold, his reward is with him, and his recompense before him."*

- ***Sermon on the Mount (Matt. 5–7):*** In Christ's longest, and most famous sermon, the theme of rewards is mentioned nine times. This is quite significant.

- ***Matthew 10:42:*** *"And whoever gives one of these little ones even a cup of cold water because he is a disciple, truly, I say to you, he will by no means lose his reward."* Christ promises to reward us even for little acts of kindness that might seem unimportant and irrelevant.

- ***The Parable of the Talents (Matt. 25:14–30):*** In this parable, Christ gave certain individuals talents (abilities, gifts, time, resources, etc.) and then went away on a long journey. Upon returning, He settled accounts with those to whom He gave the talents. Some of these servants served well and doubled their talents. To them were given rewards based on their efforts and faithfulness. For the person who was lazy and chose not to serve God—even though he knew he would incur judgment—he was punished and sent to hell. This parable teaches that God will reward those who faithfully serve Him and punish those who don't.

- ***Luke 6:23:*** *"Rejoice in that day, and leap for joy, for behold, your reward is great in heaven; for so their* *fathers did to the prophets."* God promises to reward us for enduring persecution for His name.

- **2 John 1:8:** *"Watch yourselves, so that you may not lose what we have worked for, but may win a full reward."* God promises to reward us for our works and service for Him.

- **Revelation 22:12 (NASB):** *"Behold, I am coming quickly, and **My reward is with Me**, to render to every man according to what he has done."* This verse is found just before the Bible ends. In it, Christ talks about how He will bring rewards with Him upon His return.

The doctrine of rewards is found all throughout Scripture. It teaches that how we use the abilities, gifts, time, and resources that God gives us in this life will determine the rewards we will have in the next.

Christians and Rewards at the Judgment Seat of Christ

Scripture teaches that all Christians will give an account for how they used their talents and served God at a place called the "Judgment Seat of Christ." At this place, the believer is not judged as to whether they will be saved and going to heaven, but judged based on how they used their talents and served Christ in this present life: *"For we must all appear before the judgment seat of Christ, so that each one may **receive what is due for what he has done** in the body, whether good or evil"* (2 Cor. 5:10). This passage reveals the reality that each

Chapter 4: Our Works and Service for Christ

believer will stand before Christ and give an account for how they served Him in this life, and based on how they served Him, will determine the rewards they will receive in heaven.

There's another passage that sheds light on the Judgment Seat of Christ and what will take place there. It deserves a close look as it contains sobering words we should carefully ponder:

> *According to the grace of God given to me, like a skilled master builder I laid a foundation, and someone else is building upon it. Let each one take care how he builds upon it. For no one can lay a foundation other than that which is laid, which is Jesus Christ. Now if anyone builds on the foundation with gold, silver, precious stones, wood, hay, straw — each one's work will become manifest, for the Day will disclose it, because it will be revealed by fire, and the fire will test what sort of work each one has done.* ***If the work that anyone has built on the foundation survives, he will receive a reward. If anyone's work is burned up, he will suffer loss, though he himself will be saved, but only as through fire*** (1 Cor. 3:10-15).

This passage teaches that some Christians will suffer loss when they appear before Christ to be judged for how they lived their lives and used the talents given them. They will still be saved and go to heaven, but they will suffer a loss of some kind. Some of these Christians might suffer loss because they served out of self-glory or wrong motives, and some might suffer loss because of laziness and unfruitfulness as seen in the Parable of the Talents.

Scripture teaches that heavenly rewards will be given to believers based upon their service to Christ. For those who have been diligent in serving and focused upon storing their riches in heaven, they will enjoy them forever. For those who lived carelessly, they will be saved, but will suffer a loss of some kind and have few or no rewards in heaven.

The Difference Between a Gift and a Reward

What's the difference between a gift and a reward? A gift is something freely received and isn't based upon our effort or works but upon the kindness and love of another. However, a reward is given based on our efforts and works.

Scripture clearly teaches that salvation is a gift and is not based on works or effort in any way: *"For by grace you have been saved through faith. And this is not your own doing; it is the gift of God,* **not a result of works***, so that no one may boast"* (Eph. 2:8–9). The only thing we must do to receive Christ's gift of salvation is accept it.

Rewards, on the other hand, are given by God based upon our efforts and service to Him. This is why the theme of rewards is found so abundantly throughout Scripture and why Christ so emphatically encouraged us to lay up riches in heaven.

Chapter 4: Our Works and Service for Christ

Misunderstanding Heavenly Rewards

I believe there are four main misunderstandings today that are negatively affecting the doctrine of heaven and rewards.

1. The belief that heaven and the rewards given there will be the same for everyone despite how we live our lives on earth.
2. The belief that God's grace will wipe away all the consequences of choices made in this life so we can live negligently without suffering any eternal ramifications.
3. The belief that a Christian's freedom in Christ means they have the liberty to sin without any eternal consequences and accountability.
4. The misunderstanding or denial that all believers will give an account at the Judgment Seat of Christ for how they served God with their lives and used the talents given them.

These four misunderstandings are detrimental to heavenly rewards. At stake are not trivial matters, but the loss of rewards that will affect our eternal state.

Consequences of Misunderstanding Heavenly Rewards

Because many believe in some, or all four theological fallacies mentioned, they run the danger of doing just enough to get by in their Christian lives in the present. They conclude that they're going to heaven, and heaven will be the same for everyone, so why sacrifice this life's pleasures? In their view, the important thing is just making it to heaven. So they'll tend to do just enough to get to heaven but live their lives as they wish in the present.

I believe this mentality is seriously affecting our pursuit of the true riches of life, and for this reason, we're somewhat apathetic in our Christian lives. It might explain why 81% of Evangelical Christians don't read their Bibles regularly,[3] why 61% of believers have not shared their faith in the last six months,[4] and why the average time spent in prayer is 1–7 minutes a day.[5]

After all, if how we serve God in this life doesn't really affect our life and rewards in heaven, then many will take the soft and pleasurable road instead. They'll just be content with going to heaven, believing it will be the same for everyone. As a result, the true riches of life will be neglected because they're built upon the premise that the sacrifice and effort invested in serving Christ in this life will be rewarded in heaven.

---

[3] Russ Rankin, *Study: Bible Engagement in Churchgoer's Hearts, Not Always Practiced,* Nashville, 2012, http://www.lifeway.com/Article/research-survey-bible-engagement-churchgoers, Accessed 07/23/2016.

[4] Jon D. Wilke, *Churchgoers Believe in Sharing Faith, Most Never Do,* 2012, Lifeway.com, http://www.lifeway.com/Article/research-survey-sharing-christ-2012, Accessed 08/19/2016.

[5] Deborah Beeksma, *The Average Christian Prays a Minute a Day; Prayer by the Faithful Helps Their Relationships,* GodDiscussion.com, 2013, Accessed 07/27/2015. Victory Life Church, VictoryLifeChurch.org, *Intercessory Prayer—Praying Always,* www.victorylifechurch.org/pdf/Intercessory_Praying_Always.pdf, Accessed 08/19/2016.

Chapter 4: Our Works and Service for Christ

How Many Rewards Do You Want?

The sobering reality exists that each one of us has been granted the freedom to choose the amount of rewards we will have in heaven. It's not God's choice, but ours! He will simply be faithful in rewarding us based on how we used our talents in serving Him. Some will have many rewards and enjoy them for eternity, while others will have few or no rewards and live with that reality forever. Heaven will be wonderful and the same place for every believer, but not all will enjoy the same amount of rewards there.

There are eternal consequences to the belief held by many that heaven and the eternal rewards given there will be the same for everyone. However, according to the Parable of the Talents (Matt. 25:14–30) and the Parable of the Minas (Luke 19:11–27), heaven will be the same place for all who enter, but it will not be the same experience. Some will have many rewards and be given oversight over much, while some will have few rewards and be given oversight over little or, possibly, nothing.

We Serve God Because We Love Him, Not Just to Get Rewards

I need to make it emphatically clear that we should not serve God just for His rewards, but because we genuinely love Him. God will only reward us if our motives are pure and we serve Him with grateful, overflowing love for all He has done for us.

The Distractions of Life

Many Christians are being sucked into the deception that materialism, pleasure, and prestige are more important than their eternal rewards in heaven. These distractions simply sidetrack them from the true riches of life.

The fact that most Christians don't regularly read their Bibles, have not shared their faith in the last six months, and only pray between 1-7 minutes a day reveal that many Christians are distracted and neglecting the true riches of life.

Many believers are invested so heavily in this life that they're blind to eternity. They're working so hard to have a pleasant and enjoyable life now that storing up their riches in heaven is neglected. They have the eye impediment of shortsightedness. In our unprecedented age of saturated stimuli, we're more susceptible than ever to this danger.

Following Christ means He has complete priority over our pursuits and goals. It means He is number one in our life, and not just in theory, but in reality.

Loving the World More Than God

We live in wonderful times with abundant luxuries and blessings. However, many are lost in the blessings and love this world too much. As mentioned earlier, we need to heed God's warning: *"Do not love the world or the things in the world. If anyone loves the world, the love of the Father is not in him. For all that is in the world —*

Chapter 4: Our Works and Service for Christ

the ***desires of the flesh*** *and the **desires of the eyes** and **pride of life** — is not from the Father but is from the world. And the world is passing away along with its desires, but whoever does the will of God abides forever"* (1 John 2:15-17).

While our earthly activities aren't wrong in and of themselves, they can be if we're so occupied with them that we don't have time for pursuing the true riches of life. If we're so absorbed in worldly activities that we have little time for eternal matters, then we love this world more than we should.

God loves to bless us and richly provide us with everything to enjoy (1 Tim. 6:17). However, if we focus more on the blessings of God rather than on God Himself, then it indicates we love the blessings more than God. We can become guilty of worshipping the idols of wealth, fame, and pleasure instead of God. As a result, we fail to be rich toward God and invest in our eternal home. We might be rich in earthly possessions but poor in heavenly riches.

Many Christians today are poor spiritually. They are like the lukewarm Christians in the church of Laodicea: *"For you say, I am rich, I have prospered, and I need nothing, not realizing that you are wretched, pitiable, poor, blind, and naked"* (Rev. 3:17). Many Christians are blind to their spiritual poverty, having no idea of their condition before God and of their possible loss of eternal rewards in heaven. Their eyes are locked on this world and are honed in on storing up their treasures here. Thus, they are poor and naked but don't know it.

The Cost of Materialism

Christ told a parable that perfectly illustrates the foolishness of being so absorbed in materialism and pleasure that the true riches of life are neglected:

> And he said to them, "Take care, and be on your guard against all covetousness, for one's life does not consist in the abundance of his possessions." And he told them a parable, saying, "The land of a rich man produced plentifully, and he thought to himself, 'What shall I do, for I have nowhere to store my crops?' And he said, 'I will do this: I will tear down my barns and build larger ones, and there I will store all my grain and my goods. And I will say to my soul, 'Soul, you have ample goods laid up for many years; relax, eat, drink, be merry.' But God said to him, 'Fool! This night your soul is required of you, and the things you have prepared, whose will they be?' So is the one who lays up treasure for himself and is not rich toward God" (Luke 12:15–21).

This rich man had it all. He worked hard to have a good life. In fact, he worked so hard that he reached the point of retirement where he thought it was time to reap the rewards of his labor. He said to himself, *"Soul, you have ample goods laid up for many years; relax, eat, drink, and be merry."*

His desire is really the inner desire of us all. We long for the time when we can kick back, relax, and eat, drink, and be merry.

In our Western culture, retirement is elevated as the

Chapter 4: Our Works and Service for Christ

time to eat, drink, and be merry. We're told to work hard so we can "kick back" and enjoy life during retirement. We need to be careful not to buy into our culture's message and neglect serving God in our latter years, or we might end up being fools like the rich man. Those in retirement have the most wisdom, time, and experience to offer, yet many are eating, drinking, and being merry instead of serving God.

Most Christians would strongly argue that their possessions aren't more important than God. However, the time they spend devoted to them reveals the opposite.

Physical possessions are nothing more than what allows us to exist, and our purpose for existing is to know God and attain spiritual maturity, not getting lost in materialism. If our possessions become more important than God, then they are out of balance and can become our modern-day idols.

Modern Day Fools

Christ calls those who focus primarily on this life and aren't rich toward God, fools! They work hard at acquiring a good life; they get a large house, nice cars, a good job, a good education, and gain recognition and status before others. However, they are poor in the eyes of God and will pay the consequences for all eternity. They give more importance to this life than heaven. Their aim is to accumulate money, influence, recognition, and happiness. They believe, as the rich man, that these are the true riches of life, but Jesus says to those who pursue them and neglect serving God, "You fool!"

Often, like the rich man, we're so focused on this life that we neglect storing our riches in heaven. We're not as focused on eternity as we are on our jobs, education, homes, cars, hobbies, sports, pleasures, activities, TV, Internet, Facebook, and on and on. We have time for all these activities, but don't have much time for reading our Bibles, serving the Lord, leading Bible studies, being Sunday School teachers, sharing Christ, developing our gifts and abilities, and deepening our knowledge of God.

No Second Chance

We know that heaven will be wonderful for all who enter, and God will wipe away all tears there. However, I don't believe that when we are in heaven, He will blind our eyes to the clear reality that some will have few rewards while others will have many. That reality will be obvious and will last for all eternity. For those who suffer loss (1 Cor. 3:15), they will live with that consequence forever. They will miss out on the rewards they could have had if they had not been so distracted in this present life with laying up treasures on earth instead of in heaven. This is a sobering thought that should give us great pause.

When we enter heaven, what we did in this life and how we lived it will be locked in place for all eternity. We'll have no second chance to go back and relive our lives and lay up riches in heaven as we could have.

Chapter 4: Our Works and Service for Christ

After we realize our great error, it will be too late.

The misunderstanding of heavenly rewards has huge ramifications for our eternal state. As a result, many will be deeply regretful when they appear before the Judgment Seat of Christ and suffer loss or receive few, or no rewards.

Chapter 5

True Riches #3
The Transformation of Our Nature

The transformation of our nature is also one of the true riches of life. God's desire for us is that we would become like Him in our nature, thoughts, purposes, and values.

*And we know that in all things God works for the good of those who love him, who have been called according to his purpose. For those whom he foreknew he also predestined to be **conformed to the image of his Son**, in order that he might be the firstborn among many brothers* (Rom. 8:28-29).

Transformation Is a Difficult and Painful Process

The process of being transformed into the image of Christ is difficult and painful. For this reason, many are unwilling to pay the price and choose to retain their sinful nature rather than engage in the transformation process. However, God understands this and despite our permission, puts difficult situations and issues in our lives that force us to be transformed.

It's Different Than What We Would Choose

If you were to ask me what my plans are for my life, I would include the following: I want to be well liked, popular, handsome, respected, honored, wealthy, healthy, smart, happy, and have a life of ease. I wouldn't naturally choose the difficult and painful option of being transformed into the nature of Christ. I'm sure you're probably like me as well. In truth, the transformation process rubs against the desires of our

Chapter 5: The Transformation of Our Nature

wants and wills.

Trials Teach Character Which Transforms Our Nature

Trials, problems, difficulties, and the challenges of life are some of God's choicest tools for transforming us. God highlights this in James 1:2–4:

Count it all joy, my brothers, when you meet trials of various kinds, for you know that the testing of your faith produces steadfastness. And let steadfastness have its full effect, that you may be perfect and complete, lacking in nothing.

God says that we should count it all joy when we encounter trials. That's a totally different response than what we normally have. We usually get anxious, frustrated, angry, and discouraged. Our problem is that we're short-sighted. We're just looking at life from the perspective of ease and happiness, not transformation and eternity. In fact, if we're honest, most of our prayers revolve around asking God to alleviate our trials instead of praying for steadfastness and transformation.

God says that the trials He sends us test our faith and produce strength and steadfastness. This steadfastness (perseverance and endurance) is what allows God's trials to perfect and transform us.

God also talks about the role of trials in purifying and perfecting us in 1 Peter 1:6–7:

In this you rejoice, though now for a little while, if necessary, you have been grieved by various trials, so that the tested genuineness of your faith — more precious than gold that perishes though it is tested by fire — may be found to result in praise and glory and honor at the revelation of Jesus Christ.

God allows grievous trials to test the genuineness of our faith. These trials and problems are used to transform us into the image of Christ, which is our purpose in life.

Suffering Will Make Us Grateful and Appreciate Heaven More

Life is also filled with suffering and pain. Many have a problem understanding this and turn against God. However, unless we look at life through an eternal lens, we'll get lost in this same problem as well and fail to understand God's eternal purposes for suffering. God is using suffering to transform us into His nature and gives us this insight in 2 Corinthians 4:17:

So we do not lose heart. Though our outer self is wasting away, our inner self is being renewed day by day. For this light momentary affliction is preparing for us an eternal weight of glory beyond all comparison, as we look not to the things that are seen but to the things that are unseen. For the things that are seen are transient, but the things that are unseen are eternal.

God asks us to not lose heart in the midst of our suffering in this life. For while our outward self is

Chapter 5: The Transformation of Our Nature

buffeted, God is using this process to renew us inwardly and transform us. While our suffering and affliction seems never ending and heavy, God calls it light and momentary. Then He gives us the reason for our suffering: it is preparing us an eternal weight of glory that is beyond all comparison. However, in order to cooperate with God in this process, we need to look at the unseen and eternal purposes of life rather than the temporary physical ones.

I believe part of God's purpose in allowing suffering in this life is to prepare us for heaven. Because we have suffered and experienced sin in this life, we'll be more grateful for heaven as a result. After all, do you think when you're in heaven with your perfect body, with your perfect personality, being perfectly loved and loving others perfectly, in a perfect environment with perfect people and a perfect God that you'll want to return to this life with all its pain, sinfulness, and suffering?

In a sense, God is inoculating us against sin so that we'll never have the slightest desire to return to it. We are gaining sight in this life into the destruction and ugliness sin causes. Thus, we'll be more grateful and appreciate heaven even more.

God Even Uses Evil in the Process of Transforming Us

What about evil? Does God use it in the transformation process? We began this chapter by looking at Romans 8:28 which says, *"And we know that* in **all things** *God works for the good of those who love him, who have been called according to his purpose."* This verse says that God uses **all things**. Once again, does that include evil?

I believe the answer is yes, according to Scripture. We see in the life of Joseph that he was sold into slavery by his brothers. When they were reunited in Egypt, Joseph said to them, *"As for you, you meant evil against me, but God meant it for good, to bring it about that many people should be kept alive, as they are today"* (Gen. 50:20).

The crucifixion of Christ is another example of how those who crucified Christ meant it for evil but God meant it for good. Little did Satan and the religious leaders know that God would take their evil plans and flip them into the greatest good the world has ever known, or will ever know.

However, the reality of evil presents one of the greatest problems to both Christians and non-Christians. Many ask the question, "If God is a loving God, why would He allow so much evil in life?"

What About Evil?

Did God create evil? Where did it come from? What is it? Once again, it's the most troubling question for both non-Christians and Christians. Misunderstanding the existence of evil is one of the greatest reasons many non-Christians resist God, and many Christians struggle in their faith. In order to help answer this

Chapter 5: The Transformation of Our Nature

question, the following statement is my humble definition of evil:

> Evil is a reality that exists as the result of a "being" who possesses a free will that chooses evil instead of good. God did not necessarily create evil; it's just a reality that exists as a result of any rational "being" who is endowed with a free will.

The only way to escape the reality of evil is to have beings who have no free will. However, I believe when God decided to create living beings, He chose to create them as free beings with a free will instead of creating them as puppets.

When God created living beings, He created them perfect. When He created the angels, He made them all perfect. However, Satan and a third of the angels (now called fallen angels or demons) chose evil instead.

When God created Adam and Eve, He created them perfect. However, they chose evil instead of good. As mentioned, the only way for God to have prevented angels and humans from choosing evil would have been to create them as puppets.

In addition, God is a free being who could choose evil but doesn't. So evil is just a reality that exists as the result of any intelligent being who is endowed with a free will. However, God is so big and powerful that He can even use evil in transforming us into His image: *"And we know that in **all things** God works for the good of those who love him, who have been called according to his purpose"* (Rom. 8:28).

We also struggle with evil as we live in a fallen, cursed earth. As the result of Adam and Eve's fall in the Garden of Eden, every human and all creation has been affected. Now we have diseases, sickness, death, pain, grievous work, war, famine, suffering, plagues, thorns, and a host of other bothersome problems.

God Wants to Make Us into Something Glorious

I once attended a conference that talked about how God wants to transform us into His image and make us glorious creatures. Interestingly, the speaker communicated this truth via a chalk-talk drawing. A chalk-talk is a powerful form of communication as the speaker draws a picture using a vast array of colors while speaking. Afterward, they turn special lights on the drawing, and it's transformed into a breathtaking picture with 3-D like aspects.

The speaker drew a gorgeous sunset on a beach and said, "If we'll let God do His transforming work on us through trials, suffering, pain, difficulty, and evil, then

Chapter 5: The Transformation of Our Nature

we too would become like the sunset, beautiful and gorgeous." All we need to do is cooperate with God and remain on His easel. However, if we get frustrated and give up, then we would be like a canvas jumping off the easel and refusing to be drawn upon.

I don't know if there has ever been a moment in my life when I was more inspired to let God do His perfect work within me. As the speaker finished his talk, he gave everyone an opportunity to make a commitment to cooperate with God and allow Him to transform us through His tools of trials, suffering, evil, and so on. Of course, I was totally persuaded and made this commitment.

However, after the speaker was done, he did something that caused everyone's mouth to drop to the floor. He took a big, fat, black piece of chalk and made several big lines down the picture. The audience gasped! I was shocked! The speaker had just spent an hour drawing a beautiful sunset on the beach, and then

he destroyed the picture by putting several big lines on it. I felt like yelling out, "stupid," "idiot," and so forth.

Nonetheless, the speaker was one step ahead of us and knew exactly what he was doing.

The Black Marks in Our Lives

The speaker told us that the black marks on the picture represent the painful things in our lives that, from our perspective, ruin us. We look at these black marks, such as trials, suffering, pain, and evil things that happen to us, and cry out to God, "What have You done?"

These black marks are things about our lives we cannot change! Such things like:

- *Our Appearance:* Often, we can look at ourselves and wonder why God made us the way He did. Maybe you feel you're too tall or too short. Perhaps you don't feel you are very pretty or handsome. Moreover, it could be there's something about your physical features you wish you could change, but can't.

    A number of years ago, a large number of Miss America contestants were asked, if they could, would they change their physical appearance. They all said yes. These were virtually perfect female specimens, and they still were unhappy about their physical features.

    Now I should be clear about an aspect of our appearance. If we can change something about

Chapter 5: The Transformation of Our Nature

ourselves, then it's not wrong to do so. For example, if we're out of shape, overweight, poorly groomed, and so forth, then we can, and should change these features. But regarding our unchangeable features, sometimes we look at how God has made us and see only a black mark in our lives. In many cases, if we're honest, we're deeply hurt by how God has made us.

- *Our Intelligence:* Sometimes we're unhappy with how smart God has made us. We look at others and wonder why we're not smarter. Thus, we can see our lack of intelligence as a black mark in our lives.

- *Our Personality:* This is a trait that affects many. We often feel like we don't have such a great personality. Others seem to be the life of the party, and we're just kind of fuddy-duddy. We see some of our friends or family members as popular, well-liked, highly social, and so on, and we feel inferior. We can try to change our personality, but it just doesn't work. This too can be a black mark for many.

- *Our Giftedness and Abilities:* The lack or struggle with our lack of giftedness and abilities is another area that can be a black mark in our lives. In truth, there are many people more gifted than we are, but it's also true that we are more gifted than many others. We need to ask ourselves why we desire to be gifted in the first place. Is it because we want to serve others or be served and lifted up?

Nonetheless, for many, the lack of gifts and abilities is a black mark in their lives.

- *Sickness and Pain:* All of us are affected by sickness and pain. Also, as we age and get older, sickness and pain become more common. We're all going to die, and in that process, we interface with sickness and pain. However, some are affected more. Some are born with infirmities, some have tragic things happen to them in life that causes them to lose body members, some have chronic pain and sickness, some battle with severe diseases like cancer, diabetes, and more, and some have mental and emotional issues. All this sickness and pain for many are huge black marks in their lives.

- *Family Problems:* Today, we have a crisis of epic proportions regarding the family. We have many broken homes, divorce, parents not engaged in raising their children, undisciplined children who are rebellious and unruly, and so on. All these problems provide big black marks in the lives of many. As a result, they look to the heavens and ask, "Why me? Why do I have to have these scars and black marks?"

- *Life and Death:* Life for many is not fair. Why do some die young? Why is there murder, destruction, and war? Why do some parents lose their children at young ages, and why do many of the wicked live long, full lives? All this death and pain is a black mark in the lives of many.

Chapter 5: The Transformation of Our Nature

- ***Wealth and Poverty:*** Why are some people wealthy and some people poor? Why is there so much difficulty in earning a living and surviving? Maybe you think you're poor and underprivileged, deprived of life's pleasures. Why do some seem like they're on an eternal vacation while you must sweat and toil just to get by? Being poor and struggling, for many, is a black mark in their lives.

- ***Weaknesses:*** Everyone has weaknesses in their lives. I have areas I'm weak, and you have areas you're weak. Even the Apostle Paul had weaknesses. In fact, in 2 Corinthians 12, Paul is given a thorn in the flesh that he refers to as a weakness. He prayed fervently that God would remove it. However, Scripture makes it clear that this weakness was given to Paul to keep him humble and dependent on God. After Paul had pleaded with God to remove this weakness on three distinct occasions, God told Paul, *"My grace is sufficient for you, for my power is made perfect in weakness."* Paul then responded beautifully, *"Therefore I will boast all the more gladly of my weaknesses, so that the power of Christ may rest upon me. For the sake of Christ, then, I am content with weaknesses, insults, hardships, persecutions, and calamities. For when I am weak, then I am strong"* (2 Cor. 12:9–10).

Our weaknesses and black marks can become our greatest strengths if we'll cooperate with God and let Him transform us. When we're strong in a certain area, we tend to operate in our own strength and not in the power of God's enablement. Therefore, our weaknesses have the potential of becoming our greatest strengths if we'll invite God's power into our weaknesses.

Turning Ashes to Beauty

So what did the speaker do with the big black marks on the picture that seemed to ruin it? He transformed them into stunningly, beautiful palm trees. The audience then sat in amazement! Now the picture was a hundredfold more beautiful than before. Previously, it was pretty, but now it was strikingly beautiful.

The speaker then told us about how God wants to do the same in our lives. However, for God to do His work, we need to trust Him and stay on His easel. If we

Chapter 5: The Transformation of Our Nature

jump off the easel and get frustrated with God, then the black marks will destroy us instead of transforming us.

Someone has said, "It's not so important what happens **to** us as to what happens **in** us." God's purpose in life is to transform us into His image. However, our purpose is generally to be happy and have a life of ease. These two purposes are in direct opposition. Whether we're transformed or not depends on what purpose in life we choose. If we choose to trust God with the black marks in our lives, He'll use them to make us into a gorgeous picture.

The Example of Christ in the Transformation Process

If we want to become like Christ, then most likely we'll have to endure what Christ endured. Christ was hungry, thirsty, tired, criticized, attacked, persecuted, tempted, and so on. If God allowed Christ to experience all these things, then I'm sure He will allow us to experience them as well.

Interestingly, in Hebrews 5:8-9, when speaking of Christ, it says, *"Although he was a son, he learned obedience through what he suffered. And being made perfect, he became the source of eternal salvation to all who obey him, being designated by God a high priest after the order of Melchizedek."*

We know that Christ was 100% God and 100% human. He was God in the flesh. However, in Christ's human side, He was subject to all the aspects of life we face so that He could identify with us and become our perfect, eternal High Priest. So in His human side, according to Scripture, He was made perfect through all He suffered.

In the same way as Christ, we are made perfect and transformed by God through the difficulties we suffer in life.

Our Transformed Nature Is Eternal

We won't take our possessions with us to heaven, but we will take our character, memories, experiences, and an essence of our transformed nature with us. That's why it's so important to realize that the transformation of our nature is one of God's key purposes for us in this life. If we neglect the transformation process, then we can miss an eternal benefit and reward God has for us.

Chapter 6

True Riches #4

Our Faith in God

When the winds of adversity blow hard, and life seems hard and unbearable, what will provide the steady anchor for our battered souls? Simply said, it will be our faith in God.

In the last chapter, we talked about how God uses trials, suffering, pain, evil, and so forth to transform us. However, many people bail in their faith in God when life's storms beat and batter them. They bail on God when the trials and suffering He uses to transform them are difficult to understand.

Did the Person Job, In the Bible, Have a Reason to Bail on God?

I believe God gave us the book of Job to answer the question of what to do when we don't understand life's agony and hardships. The most asked question when trials, suffering, pain, and evil deal us their stinging blows is, "Why?" The book of Job answers this question.

Who Was Job?

Job was the wealthiest man who lived in the East sometime before or around the time of Abraham. Scripture tells us about this outstanding person:

There was a man in the land of Uz whose name was Job, and that man was blameless and upright, one who feared God and turned away from evil. There were born to him seven sons and three daughters. He possessed 7,000 sheep, 3,000 camels, 500 yoke of oxen, and *500 female donkeys, and very many servants, so that this man was the greatest of all the people of the east* (Job 1:1–3).

Job was upright and blameless (not perfect, but spiritually mature and deeply devoted to obeying God in all matters of life). He had ten children and was extremely wealthy and respected. In fact, he was the greatest of all the people of the East.

What Happened to Job?

As mention, in God's desire to answer the question about trials, suffering, pain, and evil, He uses Job as an example.

In chapter one, we are privileged to get a glimpse into heaven and what is about to take place to Job. Look at this incredible scene:

Now there was a day when the sons of God came to present themselves before the Lord, and Satan also came among them. The Lord said to Satan, "From where have you come?" Satan answered the Lord and said, "From going to and fro on the earth, and from walking up and down on it." And the Lord said to Satan, "Have you considered my servant Job, that there is none like him on the earth, a blameless and upright man, who fears God and turns away from evil?" Then Satan answered the Lord and said, "Does Job fear God for no reason? Have you not put a hedge around him and his house and all that he has, on every side? You have blessed the work of his hands, and his possessions have increased in the land. But stretch out your hand and touch all that he has, and he will curse you to your face." And the Lord said to Satan, "Behold, all that he has is in your hand. Only against him do not stretch out your hand." So Satan went out from the presence of the Lord (Job 1:6–12).

Satan's accusation to God was that "The reason Job follows you is because you've bought him. Job doesn't love you because of who you are, but because of all you do for him." Satan claims that if God would only send Job some severe trials, suffering, and pain, then Job would throw in the towel, bail in his faith, and would curse God to His face.

Round One of Job's Trials

So God gives Satan permission to send Job some severe trials, but sets a limit in that Satan can't afflict Job's body with sickness. Thus, Satan looks for the opportune time and then hits Job as hard as he can. Suddenly, through various supernatural events, Satan takes away all Job has. Here are the trials God allowed Satan to inflict on Job in round one (Job 1:13–19):

- He lost all his livestock (his source of income).
- He lost all his servants (his employees).
- He lost his ten children by a supernatural wind that destroyed the house in which they were all gathered.

These were all mega-trials! Just ponder the reality of each of them. Let them sink in and think about how

Chapter 6: Our Faith in God

they would have played out.

How would Job respond? How would you respond? Here's Job's response:

> *Then Job arose and tore his robe and shaved his head and fell on the ground and worshiped. And he said, "Naked I came from my mother's womb, and naked shall I return. The Lord gave, and the Lord has taken away; blessed be the name of the Lord." In all this Job did not sin or charge God with wrong* (Job 1:20–22).

What an amazing response! After losing all his source of livelihood, his employees, and most of all, every one of his precious children at the same time, he did not bail on God and lose his faith. Job passed round one of the trials, suffering, pain, and evil that God allowed to happen to him.

Round Two of Job's Trials

Satan wasn't done yet, and neither was God. God was going to allow Job to suffer even more trials, pain, and hardship.

After Satan and God conversed about Job's response, in which God boasted to Satan about how proud He was of Job, Satan responded:

> *Then Satan answered the Lord and said, "Skin for skin! All that a man has he will give for his life. But stretch out your hand and touch his bone and his flesh, and he will curse you to your face." And the Lord said to Satan, "Behold, he is in your hand; only spare his life"* (Job 2:4–6).

God now gave Satan permission to afflict Job's body with sickness. The only limit God placed on Satan was that he couldn't take Job's life.

So Satan devised the most devastating, serious, painful affliction he could. Something that would make Job's life unbearable. He sent him excruciatingly painful boils all over his body. Deep, huge boils that oozed with puss. We should notice that Job didn't have access to painkillers like we do today. Scripture describes the scene as such:

> *So Satan went out from the presence of the Lord and struck Job with loathsome sores from the sole of his foot to the crown of his head. And he took a piece of broken pottery with which to scrape himself while he sat in the ashes* (Job 2:7–8).

What a tragic blow to Job! Not only had he lost his source of income, his employees, and all his children, but now he was in physical torment beyond measure. How would he respond to these new trials stacked on top of his previous ones? How would you respond?

To make matters even worse, while Job sat in a heap of ashes scraping his painful boils with a broken piece of pottery, his wife came to him and said, *"Do you still hold fast your integrity? Curse God and die"* (Job 2:9).

Job's wife was now throwing in the towel and bailing on her faith in God, and she was encouraging Job to do the same. But Job said to her, *"You speak as one of the foolish women would speak. Shall we receive good from God, and shall we not receive evil?"* (Job 2:10).

Chapter 6: Our Faith in God

So Job found himself in ruins. He had lost everything. He also lost the support of his wife which should have been a strong source of strength for him in his great time of need. Moreover, he knew it all didn't happen by chance. He knew very well that God was behind everything because it all happened so suddenly and supernaturally.

Then God records in Scripture His pleasure with Job and states, *"In all this Job did not sin with his lips"* (Job 2:10). Job had passed the two tests God had sent him.

Job's Friends Come to Help

While Job is in a state of pain and suffering, three of his closest friends come to visit him. When they arrive, they are speechless. They can't believe what has happened to Job. In fact, they are so stunned that they don't say anything to Job for an entire week. They just can't believe it and apparently don't know what to say. God describes the scene as such:

Now when Job's three friends heard of all this evil that had come upon him, they came each from his own place, Eliphaz the Temanite, Bildad the Shuhite, and Zophar the Naamathite. They made an appointment together to come to show him sympathy and comfort him. And when they saw him from a distance, they did not recognize him. And they raised their voices and wept, and they tore their robes and sprinkled dust on their heads toward heaven. And they sat with him on

> *the ground seven days and seven nights, and no one spoke a word to him, for they saw that his suffering was very great* (Job 2:11-13).

Job was in such a state of affliction and pain that his friends couldn't even recognize him. They were so dismayed that they wept, tore their robes, threw dust toward heaven, and sat with him for a whole week in a state of shock.

Job's Quest to Understand

Naturally, Job, like us, desire to understand the tragedies in our lives. So for the next 34 chapters of the book of Job, Job and his three friends seek to discover why God has allowed these black marks in Job's life.

Job's three friends basically attribute Job's black marks to some sin Job has in his life. Job recognizes that he's not perfect, but knows the reason is not due to sin.

After much debate, Job gets frustrated with his friends and desires to take his case to God. He becomes bold with God and asks to speak with Him face to face.

God Answers Job

God answers Job's petition to meet with Him and comes in the form of a whirlwind.

> *Then the Lord answered Job out of the whirlwind and said: "Who is this that darkens counsel by words without knowledge? Dress for action like a man; I will question you, and you make it known to me"* (Job 38:1-3).

Chapter 6: Our Faith in God

God first accuses Job of darkening counsel with words without knowledge. In other words, *"Job, you don't know very much."*

He then tells Job that if he wants to have a discussion with Him, he better *"Dress for action like a man."* This means that Job had better be prepared to have a deep, theological, informed, responsible conversation.

For the next four chapters (Job 38–41), God answers Job's questions by asking him nearly 80 questions of His own. Questions such as:

- *"Where were you when I laid the foundation of the earth? Tell me, if you have understanding. Who determined its measurements — surely you know! Or who stretched the line upon it? On what were its bases sunk, or who laid its cornerstone, when the morning stars sang together and all the sons of God shouted for joy?"*

- *"Have you commanded the morning since your days began, and caused the dawn to know its place?"*

- *"Have the gates of death been revealed to you, or have you seen the gates of deep darkness?"*

- *"Have you comprehended the expanse of the earth? Declare, if you know all this."*

- *"Where is the way to the dwelling of light, and where is the place of darkness, that you may take it to its territory and that you may discern the paths to its home? You know, for you were born then, and the number of your days is great!"*

- *"Can you send forth lightnings, that they may go and say to you, 'Here we are'?"*
- *"Is it by your understanding that the hawk soars and spreads his wings toward the south?"*

After God had asked Job about 80 questions similar to the ones above, Job responded to God:

Then Job answered the Lord and said: "I know that you can do all things, and that no purpose of yours can be thwarted. Therefore, I have uttered what I did not understand, things too wonderful for me, which I did not know. I had heard of you by the hearing of the ear, but now my eye sees you; therefore, I despise myself, and repent in dust and ashes" (Job 42:1-3; 5-6).

God answered Job's question by enlarging his view of who He was and who Job was. The more than 80 questions God asked Job served to put things in perspective. Job had a diminished view of God that needed to be enlarged. In all the dialogue between God and Job, God didn't ask Job to understand all that was happening, but rather to just have faith and trust Him.

Job's Restoration

After Job had learned the lesson God had for him, God then restored all Job had lost twofold and blessed him beyond measure. He had more sons and daughters and lived out his remaining years extremely blessed.

Chapter 6: Our Faith in God

Job 42:10–17 recounts this moving restoration:

> *And the Lord restored the fortunes of Job, when he had prayed for his friends. And the Lord gave Job twice as much as he had before. Then came to him all his brothers and sisters and all who had known him before, and ate bread with him in his house. And they showed him sympathy and comforted him for all the evil that the Lord had brought upon him. And each of them gave him a piece of money and a ring of gold. And the Lord blessed the latter days of Job more than his beginning. And he had 14,000 sheep, 6,000 camels, 1,000 yoke of oxen, and 1,000 female donkeys. He had also seven sons and three daughters. And he called the name of the first daughter Jemimah, and the name of the second Keziah, and the name of the third Keren-happuch. And in all the land there were no women so beautiful as Job's daughters. And their father gave them an inheritance among their brothers. And after this Job lived 140 years, and saw his sons, and his sons' sons, four generations. And Job died, an old man, and full of days.*

What Does Job's Life Teach Us about Faith in God?

Like Job, there are often black marks that God allows in our lives that we don't understand. Job didn't know at the time that he was on center stage in the universe before God, all the angels, Satan, and all the demons. He also didn't know that God was answering the question of why evil and hard things happen to us.

God was in the process of writing an entire book of the Bible that would be devoted to answering this question, and Job was the main actor. For all time and eternity, Job was the one God chose to teach us about evil and hardships.

Maybe God is doing the same with some of us today. Maybe we're on stage before God and others to show how God can use evil and the black marks in our lives to display God's glory as He transforms us into His nature.

Does God Ask Us to Understand Everything?

Like Job, God doesn't ask us to understand all the reasons behind what He's doing or allowing in our lives. He just asks us to have faith and trust Him. If we will, God will transform us into something beyond what we can imagine and use us as His shining trophy to show others what He can do in a life yielded to Him amidst the trials and black marks of life.

Our faith is one of the true riches that will keep us anchored during the storms of life. Many bail on God and lose their faith in Him when they don't understand what's happening, and nothing makes sense. However, God wants us to hold onto our faith tightly and never let go. It's one of our dearest and most important treasures of life.

Chapter 7

True Riches # 5

Our Knowledge of God

Discovering the True Riches of Life

Of all the true riches of life, few are as important as the knowledge of God. It's what directs us in our pursuit of the true riches of life, is how we know God, and how we understand life and the world in which we live.

Donald Whitney states, "No spiritual discipline is more important than the intake of God's Word. Nothing can substitute for it. There is simply no healthy Christian life apart from a diet of the milk and meat of Scripture."[6]

Why Is God's Word One of the True Riches of Life?

God's Word is important because it forms the foundation upon which the true riches of life rest. It's also the main component God uses in the transformation of our mind, which in turn, transforms our nature and leads to spiritual maturity.

Alister McGrath, in his article "The Passionate Intellect: Christian Faith and the Discipleship of the Mind," centers his focus of discipleship on the importance of knowledge.[7] He claims that theology was once the "queen of the sciences" and held in the highest esteem, but is no longer the case. It has declined in recent decades, and this should give us pause.[8]

---

[6] Donald Whitney, *Spiritual Disciplines for the Christian Life* (Colorado Springs: NavPress, 1991), p. 24.
[7] Alister McGrath, "The Passionate Intellect; Christian Faith and the Discipleship of the Mind" (Source: Pro Ecclesia, 22 no 1 Winter 2013, pp. 118-121. Publication Type: Review ATLA Religion Database with ATLASerials. Hunter Resource Library), Accessed 11/5/2016.
[8] Ibid., p. 118.

Chapter 7: Our Knowledge of God

McGrath believes knowledge serves believers in both their own personal understanding of God and in providing greater effectiveness in sharing this understanding with others. McGrath adds, "Christians need to realize that there is an intellectual core to the Christian faith which requires a discipleship of the mind in order to understand."[9] He further states, "Christians should be guided by a rational faith which provides the foundation for all their understanding of God and life."[10]

Knowing and Obeying God's Word Brings Success

God's Word is what brings us success in life. God says, *"This Book of the Law shall not depart from your mouth, but you shall meditate on it day and night, so that you may be careful to do according to all that is written in it. For then you will make your way prosperous, and then you will have **good success**"* (Josh. 1:8).

It's only when we know and are careful to obey God's Word that we will have success in life. Being successful in God's eyes is pursuing the true riches of life regardless of what others think.

We Are Commanded to Love the Lord with Our Minds

The greatest command is to *"Love the Lord your God with all your heart and with all your soul and **with all***

---

[9] Ibid., p. 119.
[10] Ibid., p. 119.

your mind and with all your strength" (Mark 12:30). God wants us to love Him, not only with our heart, soul, and strength, but with our minds as well. A strong case can be made that loving God begins with loving Him with our minds because it's through our knowledge of Him that we understand how to love Him with our hearts. However, many are ignorant of this truth and are biblically illiterate.

According to LifeWay Publishing, only 19% of Christians read their Bibles regularly. That leaves 81% of Christians who are basically biblically illiterate. These believers are certainly not loving God with their minds.

Christians Today and Biblical Illiteracy

Albert Mohler shares his concern about the state of evangelicalism and biblical illiteracy by asserting, "While America's Evangelical Christians are rightly concerned about the secular worldview's rejection of biblical Christianity, we ought to give some urgent attention to a problem much closer to home — biblical illiteracy in the church. This scandalous problem is our own, and it's up to us to fix it."[11]

Researchers George Gallup and Jim Castelli state the problem bluntly, "Americans revere the Bible — but, by and large, they don't read it. And because they don't

---

[11] Albert Mohler, *The Scandal of Biblical Illiteracy: It's Our Problem*, Christianity.com, http://www.christianity.com/1270946, Accessed 08/18/2016.

read it, they have become a nation of biblical illiterates. How bad is it? Researchers tell us that it's worse than most could imagine."[12]

The fact that most so-called "Evangelical believers" rarely or never read their Bibles is staggering. It's no wonder many Christians today are "throwing in" with the new progressive morals of our culture and are spiritually immature.

Christians Today and Theological Illiteracy

Not only are many believers biblically illiterate, but they are theologically illiterate as well. They don't read theological books that would significantly deepen their knowledge of God and give them a correct worldview.

God has given gifted men and women to the church who have spent countless hours studying and writing books to aid us in becoming spiritually mature. However, just a scant number of believers read theological and non-fiction Christian books. Unfortunately, most Christians are indifferent and disregard these precious gifts of God, and thus, remain spiritually immature.

The True Riches of Life Rest upon God's Word

Every aspect of the true riches of life are linked to the knowledge of God's Word. Without it, we wouldn't know who God is, who we are, who others are, the purpose for our existence, the purpose of creation,

---

[12] Ibid., Accessed 08/18/2016.

where we have come from, where we are going, what God desires from us, and how we should behave. Some downplay the importance of the knowledge of Scripture, but in so doing, contradict the value Christ gives it.

During Christ's day, discipleship had a heavy focus on the knowledge of the Bible. Most disciples had much, if not the majority of the Old Testament memorized. They would go on discipleship training trips to get away from the distractions of life and focus on learning Scripture from their rabbi.

Christ placed enormous weight upon knowing Scripture and emphasized it throughout His ministry. In fact, Scripture is so important to God that He calls Christ the "Word." *"In the beginning was the Word, and the Word was with God, and the Word was God . . . And the Word was made flesh, and dwelt among us"* (John 1:1, 14). Christ is the Living Word! To say that the knowledge of Scripture is not important is to say that Christ is not important.

Klaus Issler, in his article "Six Themes to Guide Spiritual Formation Ministry Based on Jesus' Sermon on the Mount," makes the knowledge of God's Word one of his six major themes of discipleship. He states that it was important for Jesus' disciples to know Scripture and interpret it correctly in order to be able to

Chapter 7: Our Knowledge of God

follow its genuine teaching.[13] He goes on to say, "Jesus' own life was bathed in Scripture since the phrase 'It is written' or some variation occurs 23 times on his lips."[14]

How Can We Know God?

There are two basic ways to know God: (1) by observing His creation and (2) by knowing His Word. Theologically, we call the field of knowing God through His creation "General Revelation." All rational humans can know general things about God through contemplating His creation: *"For what can be **known about God** is plain to them, because God has shown it to them. For his **invisible attributes**, namely, **his eternal power** and **divine nature**, have been **clearly perceived**, ever since the creation of the world, in the things that have been made. So they are without excuse"* (Rom. 1:19–20).

Through creation, every person knows certain truths about God. They know He is all-powerful, eternal, and all-knowing. Scripture also records in Psalm 19 that *"The heavens declare the glory of God, and the sky above proclaims his handiwork. Day to day pours out speech, and night to night reveals knowledge. There is no speech, nor are there words, whose voice is not heard. Their voice goes out through all the earth, and their words to the end of the world"* (Ps. 19:1–4). We see, then, that through creation all mankind has been blessed to know

---

[13] Klaus Issler, "Six Themes to Guide Spiritual Formation Ministry Based on Jesus' Sermon on the Mount" (Christian Ed. Journal Date: September 2010), p. 372, Accessed 11/5/2016.
[14] Ibid., p. 372.

certain things about God.

While what we can know about God through His creation is amazing, it is nonetheless, limited. We don't know the details about God, just the big picture. How can we know the details? Through learning and applying God's Word to our lives. Theologically, we call the field of knowing God through His Word "Special Revelation."

It's special because it's unique and allows us to know God in His fullness. It also gives us understanding about who we are, the purpose of life, the plan of God for His creation, and our surroundings—all extremely important things to know.

In the remainder of this section, we'll look at why knowing and applying God's Word to our lives is so essential for attaining the true riches of life.

We Follow Christ by Following His Word

When Christ says, "Follow Me," He is telling us to follow Him and His commands. The original disciples entered into 3 ½ years of intense discipleship training with Christ, and then, after His death, His Spirit was with them as they continued as His disciples. Today, Christ primarily teaches us through His Word. However, the average believer spends little time learning from Christ through His Word. Therefore, they are unable to follow Christ.

Here's the latest Bible reading statistics of

Chapter 7: Our Knowledge of God

Christians according to LifeWay Publishing:[15]

- 19% read their Bibles daily or regularly
- 26% read their Bibles a few times a week
- 14% read their Bibles once a week
- 22% read their Bibles once a month
- 18% rarely or never read their Bibles

According to these stats, 81% of Christians don't read their Bibles regularly. That's unbelievable! And of the 19% who do read their Bibles regularly, many don't study or read it in-depth. Moreover, most don't read all the Bible, but just parts of it as devotional reading.

In general, most Christians are eons away from being the kind of disciples who know and handle God's Word with precision and clarity as commanded in 2 Timothy 2:15. As a result, most Christians are babies or adolescents in their spiritual maturity and are not serious about becoming like Christ (Heb. 5:11-14). This is a severe indictment on the state of Christianity today.

If the main avenue Christ used to teach His disciples was His words, and if the main avenue today is His words as found in Scripture, then most Christians today are extremely deficient in their ability to be disciples because their knowledge of Scripture is so desperately lacking. Unlike the original disciples who had much of Scripture committed to memory, many Christians today are biblically illiterate.

---

[15] Russ Rankin, *Study: Bible Engagement in Churchgoer's Hearts, Not Always Practiced*, Nashville, 2012, http://www.lifeway.com/Article/research-survey-bible-engagement-churchgoers, Accessed 07/23/2016.

Following Christ means following His commands in Scripture. However, if we don't know His Word, we won't know His commands, so we'll be weak, ineffective Christians unable to see and attain the true riches of life. We'll grieve Christ instead of please Him.

God Expects Us to Know His Word

God instructs us in 2 Timothy 2:15 (NASB) to *"Be **diligent** to present yourself **approved** to God as a workman who does not need to be ashamed, **accurately handling the word of truth**."* God expects us to exert diligent effort in understanding and handling His Word, not indifferent and mediocre with it.

Moreover, in 2 Peter 1:5, God adds, *"For this very reason, **make every effort** to supplement your faith with virtue, and virtue with **knowledge**."* God commands us to know His Word, handle it correctly, and grow in it. In order to do this, we must be diligent and make every effort to know it.

The Importance of God's Word

As mentioned, Scripture is the most important component in understanding the true riches of life because God supernaturally uses His inspired, living words to transform us into His image and bring us to full maturity in Christ.

The following are vital functions God's Word plays in our growth in Christ:

Chapter 7: Our Knowledge of God

- **It's food for our souls:** Matthew 4:2-4 asserts, *"And after fasting forty days and forty nights, he was hungry. And the tempter came and said to him, 'If you are the Son of God, command these stones to become loaves of bread.' But he answered, 'It is written, Man shall not live by bread alone, but by every word that comes from the mouth of God.'"* Scripture is the food that feeds our souls. In the same way our body hungers, the soul of a born-again believer hungers as well. Unfortunately, according to the Bible reading stats, 81% of believers are starving their souls, and by doing so, will never reach spiritual maturity.

- **It causes us to grow in Christ:** *"But grow in the grace and knowledge of our Lord and Savior Jesus Christ"* (2 Pet. 3:18). In addition, 1 Peter 2:2 says, *"Like newborn infants, long for the pure spiritual milk, that by it you may grow up into salvation – if indeed you have tasted that the Lord is good."* Newborn infants have nothing on their minds except milk. We too, like newborn infants, should crave the Word of God so we can grow to spiritual maturity.

- **It renews our minds and changes our thinking:** Unlike any other writing known to mankind, Scripture transforms and renews our mind, which in turn, changes our behavior and leads us to spiritual maturity. Romans 12:2 declares, *"Do not be conformed to this world, but be transformed by the renewal of your mind, that by testing you may discern* *what is the will of God, what is good and acceptable and perfect."*

- **It strengthens our faith:** *"So faith comes from hearing, and hearing through the word of Christ"* (Rom. 10:17).

- **It gives us life:** *"It is the Spirit who gives life; the flesh is no help at all. The words that I have spoken to you are spirit and life"* (John 6:63). Also, Psalm 19:8 beautifully adds, *"The precepts of the Lord are right, rejoicing the heart; the commandment of the Lord is pure, enlightening the eyes."*

- **It instructs us in all matters:** *"All Scripture is breathed out by God and profitable for teaching, for reproof, for correction, and for training in righteousness, that the man of God may be complete, equipped for every good work"* (2 Tim. 3:16–17). Moreover, Psalm 119:105 states, *"Your word is a lamp to my feet and a light to my path."*

- **It protects us from sin and destruction:** King David attested, *"I have stored up your word in my heart, that I might not sin against you"* (Ps. 119:11).

- **It brings success in life:** God commanded Joshua to keep Scripture in the forefront of his life, and meditate on it always, so he would be successful: *"This Book of the Law shall not depart from your mouth, but you shall meditate on it day and night, so that you may be careful to do according to all that is written in it. For then you will make **your way***

Chapter 7: Our Knowledge of God

***prosperous**, and then you will have **good success**"* (Josh. 1:8).

How to Embed God's Word in Your Heart

The role of Scripture in the life of a believer cannot be overemphasized. There are four key methods for acquiring it: (1) through reading, (2) through hearing, (3) through study, and (4) through memorization. The first three methods are the most common, and the last method, the least.

Personally, I've made Scripture memorization a part of my life and have experienced amazing benefits and blessings as a result. Not only has it sharpened my mental capabilities, but most of all, it has embedded the Word of God in my heart. I can say from experience that there's nothing like memorizing and meditating on God's Word. It's rich, powerful, sweet, and very life changing.

Bible Intake Is Paramount

Bible intake is critical for attaining the true riches of life and should not be neglected. To the degree we allow it to dwell in us richly and transform us will be the degree to which we will attain the true riches of life. To the degree we neglect it will be the degree to which we will remain stunted in our spiritual growth and fail to attain the true riches of life.

Chapter 8

True Riches #6

Our Relationships

We all have many relationships in life. These include family members, friends, acquaintances, and even enemies. If we do have enemies, hopefully, it's for the right reasons. After all, the prophets had enemies, Christ had enemies, the apostles had enemies, and sometimes we do as well.

Our relationships are one of the true riches of life and God wants us to treat them with utmost care and respect. These relationships form what I'd like to call our "Circle of Influence." Within our particular circle, we all have power and persuasion. We can sometimes use our influence for good and sometimes for bad.

Interestingly, in the U.S. and Canada, we understand relationships differently than many other cultures around the world. We also understand our relationships very differently than the biblical culture did.

Independent Versus Interdependent Cultures

Earlier, we talked about independent and interdependent cultures. I'd like to elaborate just a little more here to better help you understand an important truth about relationships and their role as one of the true riches of life.

As mentioned, an independent culture doesn't need one another much to get by in life. They have all they need. They have their own houses, cars, tools, knowledge, skills, justice system, money, and so on.

An interdependent culture needs one another more to get by in life because they don't have all the previous

Chapter 8: Our Relationships

mentioned items an independent culture has. Everyone needs one another to get through life, and they move through life as a community, not primarily as individuals.

In an independent culture, friends are where most of the social needs are met. In an interdependent culture, family is where most of the social needs are met.

In an independent culture, friends are just friends, in an interdependent culture they are friends/resources.

Generally speaking, an independent culture doesn't value relationships as much as an interdependent culture.

Relationship Orientation in the Bible

Virtually all the Bible takes place in an interdependent culture. Thus, the importance of family played a much higher role than it does today in independent cultures.

Since the time of Abraham, the Jewish culture was family oriented. During their 400 years in Egypt, they lived as a very close-knit unit bonded together by their unique circumstances in a foreign land.

Afterward, when they wandered in the Sinai Desert for 40 years, they lived within an even closer proximity, all learning the same lessons and sharing the same experiences.

Upon settling the Promised Land, they divided the land, and each tribe received a portion to inhabit. Then, each tribe divided their allotment of land among the family units within its tribe. The land given to each family unit would then normally have remained in their possession for hundreds upon hundreds of consecutive years.

Therefore, for example, a family living in Nazareth during the time of Christ would have had their ancestors living there for countless years before them. Each family would live in family units with parents, grandparents, great-grandparents, children, brothers, sisters, aunts, and uncles, all living in the same family complex or close-by. Unlike today, where people change locations regularly and move half-way across the country, the Jews were not mobile, but instead, lived in the same town for generation after generation.

For this reason, it was virtually impossible for a Jew to exist outside the family structure in Bible times. The family was everything. It was their support system, job provider, relationship center, and emotional stability structure.

God Wants Us to Value Our Relationships

It amazes me sometimes when I observe what little it takes today to end or damage a relationship. Hurt feelings, disagreement, bitterness, being treated unfairly, and so on are just a few ways relationships can end. In our culture, we have so many social connections that sometimes our relationships are an inch deep and a mile wide. And we have no problem

Chapter 8: Our Relationships

deleting someone from our circle of influence if they make the slightest wrong move.

God wants us to value our relationships and bear with one another in love: *"Bearing with one another and, if one has a complaint against another, forgiving each other; as the Lord has forgiven you, so you also must forgive"* (Col. 3:13). We would do well to practice this admonition. Additionally, God wants us to be humble and treat others with humility and kindness: *"With all humility and gentleness, with patience, bearing with one another in love"* (Eph. 4:2).

Understanding Different Kinds of Relationships

It should be mentioned that in situations where we might have destructive relationships that are damaging us spiritually or physically, it is wise and biblical to distance ourselves from them.

Also, we should realize different kinds of relationships and how we should conduct ourselves in them. For example, we should treat our families differently than our friends, and we should operate differently with our close friends than casual acquaintances.

We should also understand that we should be kind and friendly to all, but that our close friends should not be non-Christians. God clearly warns us of the danger of wrong friendships: *"Do not be deceived: 'Bad company ruins good morals'"* (1 Cor. 15:33).

Additionally, God says that He doesn't want us to marry, date, enter into close business dealings, or have close friends who are not Christians. Consider the following:

> Do not be unequally yoked with unbelievers. For what partnership has righteousness with lawlessness? Or what fellowship has light with darkness? What accord has Christ with Belial? Or what portion does a believer share with an unbeliever? What agreement has the temple of God with idols? For we are the temple of the living God; as God said, 'I will make my dwelling among them and walk among them, and I will be their God, and they shall be my people. Therefore, go out from their midst, and be separate from them, says the Lord, and touch no unclean thing; then I will welcome you, and I will be a father to you, and you shall be sons and daughters to me, says the Lord Almighty' (2 Cor. 6:14–18).

God doesn't want us to be unequally yoked. A yoke hitched up two oxen, cows, or animals together for working purposes. Being unequally yoked refers to being bound together with someone. While God wants Christians to love and be friendly to all, He makes it clear that our close relationships should not be non-Christians unless they are within our immediate family.

God Wants Us to Speak the Truth to Our Circle of Influence

Some Christians today propose a version of love they believe is best expressed by accepting, embracing, supporting, and celebrating certain sinful lifestyles that, according to God's Word, are immoral and wrong. I believe Scripture teaches that love is best expressed by telling the truth, not by allowing a person to continue in a destructive lifestyle for which they will destroy their lives, the lives of those around them, and incur the judgment of God.

The moral issues of our day are nothing new, and the Apostle Paul had to confront them as well. Instead of approving, celebrating, remaining silent, or overlooking these issues, he dealt with them head on by stating the truth: *"Or do you not know that the unrighteous will **not inherit the kingdom of God?** Do not be deceived: neither the sexually immoral, nor idolaters, nor adulterers, nor men who practice homosexuality, nor thieves, nor the greedy, nor drunkards, nor revilers, nor swindlers will inherit the kingdom of God"* (1 Cor. 6:9).

Approving of the sinful choices of those involved in these sins would be similar to supporting an alcoholic's damaging lifestyle. We love best by speaking the truth, not by enabling people to continue their destructive activities. Unfortunately, many Christians are ashamed of the truth, remain silent, and shy away from ministering to their circle of influence for fear of losing their status or popularity.

God Wants Us to Choose His Values, Not Those of Our Circle of Influence

Many Christians today lag behind in adopting the values of their culture by just a few years. They change their message, morals, and values in order to fit in and not lose respect.

The pressure to conform to the values of our families, friends, and culture is a mounting force many Christians are fiercely battling. It's a battle between staying true to God's Word or making concessions in order to alleviate the pressure.

To relieve this tension, many Christians are choosing a path of peace and positivity over conflict and strife. They don't want negativity in their relationships, so they avoid any conflict their religious views might bring. This is not what Christ desires for us. When we conform to our circle of influence's values, we lose our ability to influence it for Christ. We're allowing just the opposite of what we should do.

God Wants Us to Be Salt in Our Circle of Influence

Christ calls us to be salt in the world: *"You are the salt of the earth, but if salt has lost its taste, how shall its saltiness be restored? It is **no longer good for anything** except to be thrown out and trampled under people's feet"* (Matt. 5:13).

What was the purpose of salt in Christ's day? It had three main functions: (1) to preserve food (2) to add flavor, and (3) to provide minerals for bodily health.

Today, we are salt by preserving the truth of God's Word instead of sacrificing it on the altar of political correctness. We are salt by adding flavor to life through demonstrating what it means to follow Christ's commands in all areas of our lives. And we are salt by providing health to our circle of influence as we speak the truth about the destructiveness and eternal consequences of sin. However, many Christians are ashamed to say anything and go against the tide of their circle of influence's values.

God Wants Us to Be Light in Our Circle of Influence

We're also called to be lights in the world: *"You are the light of the world. A city set on a hill cannot be hidden. Nor do people light a lamp and put it under a basket, but on a stand, and it gives light to all in the house. In the same way, let your light shine before others so that they may see your good works and give glory to your Father who is in heaven"* (Matt. 5:14–16).

We are called to live in such a way so that others can see the difference in our lives from those of the world. What difference should they see? They should see believers who are living pure lives according to the commandments of God, who don't just say one thing and do another, but are genuine followers of Christ. They are not hypocrites, but practice what they preach. However, numerous studies show that "Self- identified Christians are living lives indistinguishable from non-Christians."[16]

The purpose of light is to illuminate and break the darkness. We're called to be lights by knowing God's Word and shining it into our circle of influence. We're not to join the works of darkness, but reveal the evil

---

[16] C. S. Lewis Institute, *Sparking a Discipleship Movement in America and Beyond,* cslewisinstitute.org, www.cslewisinstitute.org/webfm_send/210, Accessed 08/19/2016.

deeds of our circle of influence by shining God's Word upon it: *"For at one time you were darkness, but now you are light in the Lord. Walk as children of light (for the fruit of light is found in all that is good and right and true), and try to discern what is pleasing to the Lord. Take no part in the unfruitful works of darkness, but instead, expose **them**"* (Eph. 5:8–11).

Rather than celebrate, support, or approve the works of darkness, we should expose them. We should speak the truth in love, but nonetheless, we must speak the truth. However, many Christians are not shining the light of God's Word upon the values of their circle of influence. They are afraid and remain silent. And sadly, some even join in the works of darkness, celebrating them rather than exposing and standing against them like the great prophet Isaiah did when he said, *"Woe to those who call evil good and good evil, who put darkness for light and light for darkness who put bitter for sweet and sweet for bitter"* (Isa. 5:20).

God Wants Us to Be His Faithful Voice in Our Circle of Influence

Scripture is full of examples of those who chose to please their families, friends, and culture rather than obey God. For example, Pilate chose to offer Christ up to be crucified in order to please a crowd, and Peter chose to deny Christ instead of acknowledging Him before His accusers.

On the other hand, God provides us with many examples of those who didn't bow to political pressure

Chapter 8: Our Relationships

despite the enormous tension to do so. Among them is the Prophet Micaiah. Even though he was under extreme pressure to gloss over the Word of God to protect his life, he chose to obey God instead. His incredible story is recounted in 1 Kings 22.

During Micaiah's day, King Ahab (a wicked king over the 10 northern tribes of Israel) invited King Jehoshaphat (the king of Judah, who was a godly king) to go with him to war to take the city of Ramoth-gilead, a city once belonging to Israel but now lost to another nation.

King Jehoshaphat asked King Ahab to inquire of the Lord to see whether or not God would bless their plans. So King Ahab gathered all the prophets of Israel together, and these prophets unanimously affirmed God's blessing to bring victory if they went to battle.

King Jehoshaphat, for some reason, still had doubts and asked if there was any other prophet who could inquire of the Lord about their mission. King Ahab said, "There's this prophet Micaiah, but he never prophesies anything good from the Lord concerning me." Nonetheless, King Jehoshaphat insisted that this man be brought forth.

An officer, sent to summon Micaiah, warned the prophet not to stir up trouble by saying anything that differed from what the other prophets had already spoken. Micaiah responded, *"As the Lord lives, what the Lord says to me, that I will speak"* (1 Kings 22:14).

So Micaiah stood in the presence of King Ahab, King Jehoshaphat, all the prophets of Israel, all the officials of the two king's royal courts, and probably many army officials and commanders as well. All the power of two kingdoms were represented in this gathering. What would Micaiah do? What would he say? Would he be loyal to God and speak His words or yield to the pressure of those present and save his life? What would you do?

Micaiah chose to speak the truth of God's Word into his culture and, as a result, was scorned and beaten by the other prophets and then thrown into a dungeon by King Ahab. Nonetheless, Micaiah's words came true, and King Ahab lost his life because he refused to listen to Micaiah and the Word of the Lord.

Many other prophets in the Old Testament also spoke the Word of God to their culture and were beaten, persecuted, and killed. And the greatest example of all is Christ. He spoke the truth of God's Word into His culture and lost His life as a result.

In addition, the Apostle Paul, the apostles, and many others in Scripture suffered great persecution for standing up for God and the truth. We applaud and admire them! However, when it gets closer to home and affects us, many run from persecution and choose the values of our culture instead of standing with Christ. It's hard to stand against the tide of our culture, and it's especially hard to stand against family and friends.

Nonetheless, we have a choice to make. We can be like Micaiah, who chose to speak the Word of the Lord regardless of the cost, or we can choose the safe, easy

Chapter 8: Our Relationships

route and appease our culture. What choice will you make?

Are We Fearful of Losing Family and Friends in Our Circle of Influence?

We naturally love our family, friends, and church family, and don't want to lose them. They provide us with the relationships we so desperately need. However, we must make a choice. Will we love family, friends, and our circle of influence's values more than God? Will we remain silent on biblical issues out of fear of losing relationships? Will we conform to our society instead of being conformed to Christ? Will we fear being labeled intolerant, judgmental, dogmatic, and even hateful for speaking the truth? Will we be ashamed of what God says about moral issues and biblical truths, or will we speak the truth in love to our circle of influence?

Recall what Christ said, *"For whoever is **ashamed of me and of my words** in this adulterous and sinful generation, of him will the Son of Man also be ashamed when he comes in the glory of his Father with the holy angels"* (Mark 8:38).

Unless we want to suffer shame and embarrassment before Christ, we need to be faithful in saying what God says about our culture. We're His mouth and voice. Unfortunately, many Christians are ashamed to be fully devoted disciples as it causes problems in their relationships.

One of the ways we show our love and devotion to

Christ is by being faithful to what He teaches in His Word. By holding fast to His teachings, regardless of the pressure to do otherwise, we demonstrate our love and devotion to Christ. Christ said, *"Whoever has my commandments and keeps them, he it is who loves me"* (John 14:21).

If we don't keep Christ's commands, we have little right to claim we love Him. We can raise our hands in church, close our eyes in worship, and say whatever we want, but it's in our actions and commitment to Christ's commandments that we truly display our love for Him.

God Wants Us to Be Small "p" Prophets in Our Circle of Influence

We are, in a sense, called to be similar to the prophets of old. These prophets were called to speak God's Word to their culture. However, their hearers didn't want to hear their words and most of the prophets suffered great persecution or were killed for speaking the truth.

Today, I believe we're called to be like the prophets and speak the Word of God into our culture and circle of influence. However, the words we should speak are the words of God already revealed in Scripture, not our own beliefs and thoughts. Let me be clear: we don't speak our own words, but the words of Scripture! They are the only authoritative and inspired words known to mankind. Sadly, our culture, like the culture of the prophets, doesn't want to hear that they are sinners and their lifestyles are wrong.

Chapter 8: Our Relationships

Instead of hearing God's Word with open arms and repenting, our culture tends to get angry and attack the messenger. Nonetheless, our calling is to be small "p" prophets. We don't make up new Scripture, we just faithfully repeat what has already been revealed.

We are also not to water it down, change its nuances, alter it, or adapt it so that it blends in with our culture's values. Instead, we are to speak the truth in love. We don't concern ourselves with how those in our culture might respond. How they do so is between them and God. We are called to be like the Prophet Ezekiel:

> *So you, son of man, I have made a watchman for the house of Israel. Whenever you hear a word from my mouth, you shall give them warning from me. If I say to the wicked, O wicked one, you shall surely die, and you do not speak to warn the wicked to turn from his way, that wicked person shall die in his iniquity, but his blood I will require at your hand. But if you warn the wicked to turn from his way, and he does not turn from his way, that person shall die in his iniquity, but you will have delivered your soul* (Ezek. 3:17–19).

God told Ezekiel that He would hold him accountable if he didn't faithfully warn the wicked people of his day to turn from their sins. I believe God will hold us accountable as well if we don't do the same. If we smooth over the sins of our culture or remain silent because we're afraid, then I believe God will hold us accountable.

Why do many Christians remain silent and don't speak the words of God into their culture or circle of influence? Possibly, it's because they fear being labeled intolerant, judgmental, dogmatic, or hateful. Certainly, that's what every culture in the Bible said to those who spoke God's Word to them as well. Whether it was the prophets, Christ, the apostles, or us, it always has been, and will always be, the same.

A sinful society just doesn't want to be told that what they are doing is wrong and sinful. Therefore, when we speak God's words to them, they will naturally respond by accusing us of being intolerant, judgmental, dogmatic, or hateful. They'll attack the messenger who bears the message instead of heeding their warnings and repenting.

Sadly, many Christians are choosing to go along with our culture's sinful lifestyles because they are unwilling to be different and stand with God. Rather than being fully devoted followers of Christ, they settle for a mild version of Christianity that complies with their culture's values.

God Wants Us to Use Good Judgment in Our Circle of Influence

One of the most misunderstood verses in the Bible is *"Judge not that you be not judged"* (Matt. 7:1). It's spoken so frequently that many believe we can't say anything contrary about anyone's sinful behavior or we're guilty of judging them. They claim it doesn't matter what God's Word might say; we have no right

Chapter 8: Our Relationships

to weigh in on any matter.

What does this verse about judging really mean? We must see it in its context to fully understand it, as a verse taken out of context becomes a pretext. In other words, a verse lifted out of the other verses around it becomes what we want it to say rather than what it truly says. Here's the context:

> *Judge not, that you be not judged. For with the judgment you pronounce you will be judged, and with the measure you use it will be measured to you. Why do you see the speck that is in your brother's eye, but do not notice the log that is in your own eye? Or how can you say to your brother, "Let me take the speck out of your eye," when there is the log in your own eye? You hypocrite, first take the log out of your own eye, and **then you will see clearly to take the speck out of your brother's eye*** (Matt. 7:1–5).

First of all, it's true that our role is not to pass sentence upon another, that's God's job. However, in this passage, Jesus is not saying that we should never make any judgment about right and wrong. He means that we should not do it in a hypocritical manner.

God clearly calls us to use good judgment about right and wrong. Note how the passage ends: *"You hypocrite, first take the log out of your own eye, and then you will **see clearly** to take the speck out of your brother's eye"* (Matt. 7:5).

Therefore, this passage is **not** saying we are not to use good judgment, but instead, that we are **not** to use our judgment hypocritically. We shouldn't say, "Don't do that," while we do the very same thing. It's failing to practice what we preach.

The point of this verse is to teach us how to judge correctly, not that we can't speak the truth of Scripture regarding sinful matters. For this reason, we are given the responsibility to judge between right and wrong, but must first get the beam out of our own eye in order to see clearly.

There are other verses in Scripture that also teach we have a responsibility to judge correctly using the Word of God in dealing with others. Consider the following verses:

- **Galatians 6:1:** *"Brothers, if anyone is caught in any transgression, you who are spiritual should restore him in a spirit of gentleness. Keep watch on yourself, lest you too be tempted."*

- **1 Corinthians 5:11–13:** *"But now I am writing to you not to associate with anyone who bears the name of brother if he is guilty of sexual immorality or greed, or is an idolater, reviler, drunkard, or swindler – not even to eat with such a one. For what have I to do with judging outsiders? Is it not those inside the church **whom you are to judge?** God judges those outside. Purge the evil person from among you."*

These verses affirm that we have a responsibility to evaluate right and wrong in order to minister God's Word to others.

We must remember that to simply repeat what God

says is not being judgmental. We are not passing judgment on others when we proclaim what God's Word says to them; it is God's Word that is passing the judgment. Therefore, we must not be afraid to exercise good judgment in order to help others in our circle of influence. We are to be like doctors who prescribe medicine (God's truth) based on our patient's needs.

God Wants Us to Understand the Nature of Truth

Going back in history just a few decades and we find that the big sins were murder, adultery, stealing, lying, deception, and so on. Today, things have drastically changed. The big sins now are being intolerant, judgmental, dogmatic, believing in absolute truth, and being unaccepting of all lifestyles and choices people choose.

Truth by nature is intolerant, judgmental, dogmatic, absolute, and unaccepting of all lifestyles and choices. Things are backward today from God's standards. This shouldn't surprise us as God said in the last days this would be the case:

But understand this, that in the last days there will come times of difficulty. For people will be lovers of self, lovers of money, proud, arrogant, abusive, disobedient to their parents, ungrateful, unholy, heartless, unappeasable, slanderous, without self-control, brutal, not loving good, treacherous, reckless, swollen with conceit, lovers of pleasure rather than lovers of God, having the appearance of godliness, but denying its power. Avoid such people (2 Tim. 3:1–5).

The beliefs of the last days will even affect Christians. It says that some will have an appearance of godliness but deny its power. I believe this reference to "power" can also include the truthfulness of Scripture.

Today, many Christians are believing the same standards of the world and claiming they're following God's Word. For example, they feel that in order to love someone they need to approve and support them in their sinful lifestyles. They believe you can't tell anyone what God says about their sinful choices or you're being judgmental and unloving.

We must understand that truth by its nature is intolerant, judgmental, dogmatic, and absolute. Sadly, however, only half of Christians believe in absolute moral truth.[17] This reveals that for around half of Christians our culture's values have more influence over them than Scripture.

If I were to say, "Gravity exists, and if you jump out a window you will fall," that statement would be intolerant, judgmental, dogmatic, and absolute. However, even though some might think my statement is too dogmatic and absolute, what they think doesn't change the reality that gravity exists, and if you jump out a window, you will fall. My statement simply defines the essence of gravity.

---

[17] C. S. Lewis Institute, *Sparking a Discipleship Movement in America and Beyond,* cslewisinstitute.org, www.cslewisinstitute.org/webfm_send/210, Accessed 08/19/2016.

Chapter 8: Our Relationships

And so it is with the essence of truth. Truth cannot be truth if it's not absolute. However, in our day of relativism (the belief that there are no absolutes), truth doesn't fit well. Nonetheless, it doesn't matter at all if the majority of people think gravity doesn't exist—it still exists. And it doesn't matter what they say or how angry they may get, gravity is an absolute, intolerant, dogmatic reality. Truth is the same!

If we repeat the words of Christ, *"I am the way, and the truth, and the life. No one comes to the Father except through me"* (John 14:6), we are repeating an intolerant, judgmental, dogmatic, and absolute statement. However, we are not passing judgment and setting up our own standard of right and wrong, but just simply repeating God's divinely revealed truth.

Are We Ashamed of the Gospel?

Today, some Christians are ashamed of the gospel of Jesus Christ. For this reason, they omit parts of it that are unappealing to non-Christians. Aspects that are largely omitted or neglected include truths like the sinfulness and depravity of mankind, the consequences of sin, confession of sin, repentance, the judgments of God, the fear of the Lord, discipleship, denying self, taking up your cross, and hell. They pass over these uncomfortable truths and rush to the blessings of salvation instead. They focus on the benefits of receiving Christ but leave out the consequences of rejecting Him.

Are they ashamed of Christ and attempting to

remove the "offense of the gospel"? Interestingly, unlike many Christians today, Christ focused more on the judgments of God and the cost of following Him than the blessings.

The Apostle Paul was persecuted all over the known world because the gospel he preached was offensive: *"But if I, brothers, still preach circumcision, why am I still being persecuted? In that case, the **offense of the cross** has been removed"* (Gal. 5:11). When Christ and the apostles preached the gospel, it was very offensive to many at that time.

The gospel was offensive to the Jews who believed that following the Law brought salvation. It was offensive to the Romans who believed in many false gods, and therefore, rejected the claim that salvation was found only in Christ. The gospel was folly to the secular mind who considered it ridiculous (1 Cor. 1:18). It was foolish to the Greeks who thought salvation came through wisdom and knowledge, and it's offensive to our culture today for many of the same reasons. There's no way to remove the offense of the Cross except by changing it to appease others. Unfortunately, some Christians and churches are doing just that. However, in so doing, they are proclaiming a different gospel.

According to Scripture, a gospel that omits or alters the sinfulness of mankind, who Christ is, the judgment of God, and hell is an incomplete gospel. It's a false gospel that fails to communicate that from which a person is saved. It's a false gospel similar to cults like the Jehovah Witnesses, Mormons, Seventh-Day Adventists, and others who don't believe in the judgments of God and hell.

Our Circle of Influence Needs Us

God wants us to sincerely love those within our circle of influence. However, we must understand the nature of true love. True love is willing to speak the truth and genuinely help others. It doesn't idly stand by and let others destroy themselves by allowing them to engage in sinful lifestyles. It values those within its circle of influence and seeks to guide them with the truth of God's Word. True love *"Does not rejoice at wrongdoing, but rejoices with the truth"* (1 Cor. 13:6).

Chapter 9

True Riches # 7

Godly Character

Character is one of the true riches of life and has been largely overlooked today. It's a foundational aspect of who we are and I believe will be somewhat eternal to us in nature. For these reasons, it's extremely important.

Character Is Foundational

In biblical times, knowledge was built upon the foundation of Scripture and godly character. Critical character traits like being truthful, trustworthy, honest, loyal, self-disciplined, hardworking, generous, responsible, orderly, cleanly, organized, dependable, faithful, diligent, steadfast, patient, respectful, and so on formed the foundation upon which knowledge rested.

One of the ways character was taught was by using the book of Proverbs. It was employed in Israel's educational system, and the study of it was a required subject.

The overall theme of Proverbs deals with character development. Its opening introduction states its purpose: *"To know wisdom and instruction, to discern the sayings of understanding, to receive instruction in **wise behavior**, **righteousness**, **justice** and **equity**; to give **prudence** to the naive, to the youth knowledge and discretion"* (Prov. 1:2–4, NASB). In these verses, wise behavior, righteousness, justice, equity, and prudence are foundational character traits.

I have come to the firm conclusion that character is more important than skills, giftedness, knowledge,

Chapter 9: Godly Character

social skills, and other important traits. Character is what determines how all our abilities are used, for either good or bad, and is the structure upon which abilities hang.

For example, a person could be extremely gifted musically, but if they don't have the character of self-discipline to practice, the conviction to produce wholesome music, integrity in their financial dealings, and a commitment to humility amidst success, they will be a total failure, causing severe damage to themselves and others. Abilities and knowledge can be acquired if we have good character, but without it, life comes crumbling down.

What Is Character?

Character can be defined as inner traits we possess, aspects of our nature, our moral fiber, and our foundational makeup and essence. It's who we are and what we do in secret when no one is watching. Furthermore, our convictions and decisions are controlled by it.

In Scripture, several Greek words are used interchangeably in reference to character. The following are their usages:

1. *Dokimēn*: meaning approved, tried character.
2. *Ethē*: referring to morals.
3. *Aretēn*: meaning a virtuous course of thought,

feeling and action, virtue, and moral goodness.[18]

Interestingly, the word "virtue" is commonly used in the Bible when referring to character. It's an old English word translated by some newer Bible versions as "excellence." In Scripture, the word "godliness" is also used when referring to character.

Abraham Lincoln said, "Reputation is the shadow. Character is the tree."[19] Another author has stated, "Our character is much more than what we try to display for others to see; it is who we are even when no one is watching. Good character is doing the right thing because it is right to do what is right."[20] And Thomas Babington Macauley claims, "The measure of a man's character is what he would do if he knew he would never be found out."[21]

Character Is Part of God's Essence

God uses the essence of His character as a foundational reason for trusting Him when making covenants and promises with mankind: *"The sovereign Lord confirms this oath by his own holy **character**: 'Certainly the time is approaching when you will be carried away in baskets, every last one of you in fishermen's pots'"* (Amos 4:2, NET).

---

[18] Bible Hub, *703. Arête*, http://biblehub.com/greek/703.htm, Accessed 10/23/2016.
[19] Character-training.com/blog, *What is Character?* http://www.character-training.com/blog, Accessed 10/23/2016.
[20] Ibid., Accessed 10/23/2016.
[21] Ibid., Accessed 10/23/2016.

Chapter 9: Godly Character

The Apostles Spread the Gospel Utilizing Godly Character

When the gospel was spread to the nations, the Apostle Paul said they brought it with deep conviction and character: *"We know, brothers and sisters loved by God, that he has chosen you, in that our gospel did not come to you merely in words, but in power and in the Holy Spirit and with **deep conviction** (surely you recall the **character** we displayed when we came among you to help you)"* (1 Thess. 1:4–5, NET).

Why Is Character Important?

God elevates character as an essential component of life as it's the rudder that guides and steers us. Notice that virtually every characteristic listed in 2 Peter 2, is a character trait or an attitude:

> *But also for this very reason, giving all diligence, add to your faith virtue [character], to virtue knowledge, to knowledge self-control, to self-control perseverance, to perseverance godliness, to godliness brotherly kindness, and to brotherly kindness love. For if these things are yours and abound, you will be neither barren nor unfruitful in the knowledge of our Lord Jesus Christ* (2 Pet. 1:5–8, NKJV).

This is a key passage we must take seriously. It outlines a process that leads to spiritual maturity and fruitfulness. It mentions three essential components: (1) virtue (character) (2) knowledge, and (3) attitudes.

Developing Character Takes Time

Character is built over the long haul and is not an overnight process. God uses trials, suffering, persecution, and testing to develop His bedrock character within us. He wants us to be like Him, and He is a God of impeccable character.

Romans 5:3-4 says, *"Not only that, but we rejoice in our sufferings, knowing that suffering produces endurance, and endurance produces **character**, and **character** produces hope."*

James also speaks of its importance when he says, *"Count it all joy, my brothers, when you meet trials of various kinds, for you know that the testing of your faith produces **steadfastness** [character]. And let steadfastness have its full effect, that you may be perfect and complete, lacking in nothing"* (Jam. 1:2-4).

Peter echoes the same theme as well: *"Such trials show the proven **character** of your faith, which is much more valuable than gold – gold that is tested by fire, even though it is passing away – and will bring praise and glory and honor when Jesus Christ is revealed"* (1 Pet. 1:7, NET).

Character Is the Main Quality Required in Leaders

Character is so important that it's the primary quality required in church leaders: *"Therefore, an overseer must be above reproach, the husband of one wife, sober-minded, self-controlled, respectable, hospitable, able to teach, not a drunkard, not violent but gentle, not quarrelsome, not a lover of money . . . He must not be a recent convert, or he may become puffed up with conceit and fall into the condemnation of the devil"* (1 Tim. 3:2–3, 6). This list contains many character qualities.

How to Develop Character

Greg S. Baker claims, "Building good character is all about addition, not subtraction. What I mean is this: when it comes to change, our focus is usually on the aspects of our lives that are bad. We try to cut out or cut off these negative or bad qualities. We try to improve by subtraction. That is not how you build good character. It is the process of addition in your life that brings the character. In so doing, you automatically take care of the other negative aspects."[22] Baker adds, "The Bible teaches us this concept in 2 Peter 1:5–9. We are to add things like virtue, patience, love, kindness, faith, and so on. It is the process of adding these things to our lives that we gain the character to be fruitful in life."[23] Baker concludes, "So how do we develop godly character in our lives? You practice it until it becomes part and parcel with you. You diligently focus on what you want to add and then practice it until it becomes a habit."[24]

On occasion, however, building character might

---

[22] Greg S. Baker, "How to Build Good Character," SelfGrowth.com, www.selfgrowth.com/articles/how_to_build_good_character, Accessed 11/14/2016.
[23] Ibid., Accessed 11/14/2016.
[24] Ibid., Accessed 11/14/2016.

include ceasing wrong activities in conjunction with building good character. Scripture says that we are to put off our old self and put on the nature of Christ:

Put off your old self, which belongs to your former manner of life and is corrupt through deceitful desires, and to be renewed in the spirit of your minds, and to put on the new self, created after the likeness of God in true righteousness and holiness (Eph. 4:22–24).

In this passage, we see both putting off and putting on. Therefore, in some situations, we might need to cease certain negative activities in conjunction with building godly character.

Build Godly Character

Character is a foundational aspect of who we are and takes a lifetime to build. It's part of God's essence and should be part of ours as well. Therefore, we should give utmost importance to developing character as it's one of the principle components of the true riches of life.

As mentioned, some of the more important character traits we should develop include being truthful, trustworthy, honest, loyal, self-disciplined, hardworking, generous, responsible, orderly, cleanly, organized, dependable, faithful, diligent, steadfast, patient, and respectful.

With good character, we will have success in all we attempt, but without it, all of life will come crumbling down.

Chapter 10

True Riches # 8

Godly Attitudes

Many years ago, I was involved in a children's ministry program in a church I attended and was continually puzzled by the leader's poor attitudes. She had been a believer for many years, was knowledgeable in Scripture, and appeared to be spiritually mature. Yet, she was grumpy, rude, harsh, and unpleasant. I wrestled with how this could be. As a young believer, it was all so conflictive. How could she overlook a major theme of Scripture, and why would her church put her in a leadership position having such great deficiencies in her attitudes?

Our attitudes determine how we treat and view others, God, and life. Someone has said, "A bad attitude is like a flat tire. You can't go anywhere until you change it." With good attitudes, we will have success in life, but with bad attitudes, failure.

Defining Attitudes

Attitudes can be defined as a mental state of mind, a way of thinking, a feeling, a way of behaving, a disposition, a demeanor, or an emotional state of being. Attitudes can be both positive and negative. They are the expression of our inner thoughts, feelings, emotions, beliefs, and values. Without exception, we always have some kind of an attitude.

Attitudes are the living outflow of our lives and always manifest themselves in a certain action or behavior. We will act a certain way depending on what kind of attitude we have at that time. Our attitudes are the reason we do what we do, obey or disobey, or feel

Chapter 10: Godly Attitudes

what we feel. They are the servants of our will and affect how we interact and treat others.

Biblical Attitudes in Scripture

We see both positive and negative attitudes all throughout Scripture. Galatians 5:22-23 lists several positive attitudes: *"But the fruit of the Spirit is love, joy, peace, patience, kindness, goodness, faithfulness, gentleness, self-control."*

Despite the likelihood of being in a cold prison cell in Rome, the Apostle Paul's main theme of the book of Philippians is joy. Not only was Paul joyful, but he saw it as an essential part of our Christian life: *"Convinced of this, I know that I will remain and continue with you all, for your progress and joy in the faith"* (Phil. 1:25).

Philippians 2:5-8 (NASB) tells us to have the same attitude of humility as Christ: *"Have this **attitude** in yourselves which was also in Christ Jesus, who, although He existed in the form of God, did not regard equality with God a thing to be grasped, but emptied Himself, taking the form of a bond-servant, and being made in the likeness of men. Being found in appearance as a man, He humbled Himself by becoming obedient to the point of death, even death on a cross."*

Jesus also demonstrated the role of spiritual attitudes in His life. One author has noted, "He maintained a perfect attitude in every situation because He prayed about everything and worried about nothing. Jesus' attitude was never to become defensive, discouraged, or depressed because His goal was to please the Father rather than to achieve His own agenda. In the midst of trials, Jesus was patient. In the midst of suffering, He was hopeful. In the midst of blessing, He was humble. Even in the midst of ridicule, abuse, and hostility, He 'made no threats ... and did not retaliate. Instead, He entrusted Himself to Him who judges justly.'"[25]

In the Sermon on the Mount, Christ speaks of key attitudes He wants us to possess such as being poor in spirit, meek, righteous, merciful, pure, peacemakers, and having a willing attitude towards persecution.

Negative Attitudes

There are also many negative attitudes mentioned in Scripture that God commands us to avoid. In 2 Timothy 2:3, it states, *"But understand this, that in the last days there will come times of difficulty. For people will be lovers of self, lovers of money, proud, arrogant, abusive, disobedient to their parents, ungrateful, unholy, heartless, unappeasable, slanderous, without self-control, brutal, not loving good."*

Galatians 5:19-21 also mention several negative attitudes: *"Now the works of the flesh are evident: sexual immorality, impurity, sensuality, idolatry, sorcery, enmity, strife, jealousy, fits of anger, rivalries, dissensions, divisions, envy, drunkenness, orgies, and things like these."*

---

[25] Gotquestions.org, *What Does the Bible Say About Attitude?* www.gotquestions.org/Bible-attitude.html, Accessed 10/23/2016.

Chapter 10: Godly Attitudes

Attitudes Are a Choice

We have a choice in what kind of attitude we have at any given point in time, and the attitude we choose affects all factors of life.

Chuck Swindoll highlights the value of choosing the right attitudes: "This may shock you, but I believe the single most significant decision I can make on a day-to-day basis is my choice of attitude. It is more important than my past, my education, my bankroll, my successes or failures, fame or pain, what other people think of me or say about me, my circumstances, or my position. Attitude is that 'single string' that keeps me going or cripples my progress. It alone fuels my fire or assaults my hope. When my attitudes are right, there's no barrier too high, no valley too deep, no dream too extreme, no challenge too great for me."[26]

Without Right Attitudes, We Are Nothing

Our attitudes are the visible expression of our inner thoughts, feelings, emotions, beliefs, and values. They directly affect how we interact and treat both God and others, either positively or negatively.

The true riches of life are linked to our good attitudes, and without them, God says we are nothing. This truth is strongly emphasized in 1 Corinthians 13:1–3: *"If I speak in the tongues of men and of angels, but have not love, I am a noisy gong or a clanging cymbal.*

---

[26] Chuck Swindoll, *Strengthening Your Grip* (Word Books, Waco, TX, 1982), pp. 205-206.

Discovering the True Riches of Life

*And if I have prophetic powers, and understand all mysteries and all knowledge, and if I have all faith, so as to remove mountains, but have not love, **I am nothing**. If I give away all I have, and if I deliver up my body to be burned, but have not love, **I gain nothing**."*

Chapter 11

True Riches # 9

Spiritual Maturity

Today, we have many ways of defining success in life. Some define it as being a sports hero, others as being wealthy, others as being popular and well liked, and still others as being happy. How does God define success? He defines it as being spiritually mature!

Spiritual maturity is one of the true riches of life because it's our purpose in life, not happiness, pleasure, possessions, prestige, or the fulfillment of our dreams.

What Is Spiritual Maturity?

Spiritual maturity is not perfection, but the attainment of fullness, completeness, adulthood, or excellence in the Christian life.

Christ highlighted obedience as an overarching aspect of spiritual maturity in the Great Commission Mandate: *"Teaching them to **observe all that I have commanded you.** And behold, I am with you always, to the end of the age"* (Matt. 28:20). Spiritual maturity, according to Christ, is summed up by complete obedience to all of Scripture.

The Apostle Peter focused on knowledge, attitudes, and character as essential to spiritual maturity: *"For this very reason, make every effort to supplement your faith with **virtue**, and **virtue** with **knowledge**, and **knowledge** with **self-control**, and **self-control** with **steadfastness**, and **steadfastness** with **godliness**, and **godliness** with **brotherly affection**, and **brotherly affection** with **love**"* (2 Pet. 5–7).

In addition to Christ's and Peter's definition of

Chapter 11: Spiritual Maturity

spiritual maturity, the Apostle Paul defines spiritual maturity as:

1. A person who can understand and receive the wisdom of God from Scripture: *"Yet among the **mature** we do impart wisdom, although it is not a wisdom of this age or of the rulers of this age, who are doomed to pass away"* (1 Cor. 2:6).

2. A person who is mature in their thinking capabilities: *"Brothers, do not be children in your thinking. Be infants in evil, but in **your thinking be mature**"* (1 Cor. 14:20).

3. A person who has arrived at the measure of the full stature of Christ: *"Until we all attain to the unity of the faith and of the knowledge of the Son of God, to **mature** manhood, to the measure of the stature of the **fullness** of Christ"* (Eph. 4:13).

4. A person who can discern good from evil through the constant practice of using God's Word, and can understand and feed on the solid food (deep things) of Scripture: *"But solid food is for the **mature**, for those who have their powers of discernment trained by constant practice to distinguish good from evil"* (Heb. 5:14).

5. A person with a transformed mind: *"Do not be conformed to this world, but be transformed by the renewal of your mind, that by testing you may discern what is the will of God, what is good and acceptable and **perfect**"* (Rom. 12:2). This verse presents two

options for each person: (1) be conformed to this world or (2) be transformed by Scripture to God's perfect will. Spiritual maturity is the process of moving from the conformity of this world to the conformity of God's will.

A spiritually mature person thinks as God thinks, acts like God acts, and values what God values. They have the same characteristics, attitudes, beliefs, and perspective of life that God has. They are led by the Spirit and submit to Him in all things. They love the Lord their God with all their heart, soul, mind, and strength, and they love their neighbor as themselves.

In summary, a spiritually mature person is someone who has arrived at fullness, excellence, and completeness in the Christian life. It describes a person who has their eyes set on the true riches of life and is pursuing them diligently.

Spiritual Maturity Is God's Purpose for Us

As mentioned, it's important to note that spiritual maturity is not the same as perfection. We will never reach that level in this life. However, it's a state of maturity that reflects, by and large, the image of Christ and His values. It's not like a popular bumper sticker that reads, "Not perfect, only forgiven." While this slogan contains some truth, it overlooks the majority of our Christian growth to maturity after forgiveness and makes an excuse for bad behavior in the meantime.

Between being forgiven for our sins at salvation,

Chapter 11: Spiritual Maturity

and spiritual maturity, lies a wide gap. This gap is where we labor with the grace of God to attain spiritual maturity. We all begin as spiritual infants at salvation but shouldn't stay there. We are called to much more than forgiveness; we are called to attain spiritual maturity. This is our goal and purpose in life: *"Until we all attain to the unity of the faith and of the knowledge of the Son of God, to **mature manhood**, to the measure of the stature of **the fullness of Christ**"* (Eph. 4:13).

God's desire is that we would attain spiritual maturity. In fact, He sharply rebukes those who are slow or fail to attain it as seen in Hebrews 5:11–14:

> *About this we have much to say, and it is hard to explain, since you have become **dull of hearing**. For though **by this time** you ought to be teachers, you need someone to teach you again the **basic principles** of the oracles of God. You **need milk**, not solid food, for everyone who lives on milk is **unskilled** in the word of righteousness, since he is a **child**. But solid food is for the mature, for those who have their powers of discernment trained by constant practice to distinguish good from evil.*

God was angry and rebuked these Hebrew believers because they were slothful in attaining spiritual maturity. God feels the same about us today! He expects us to become spiritually mature within a reasonable length of time and is grieved when we fail to do so.

God was also grieved with the nation of Israel for

the same reasons: *"But they obeyed not, neither inclined their ear, but made their neck stiff, that they might not hear, nor receive instruction"* (Jer. 17:23).

Few Attain Spiritual Maturity

Spiritual maturity is an overlooked purpose in life and few attain it. Every person begins their Christian life as a spiritual baby. That's fine. However, the tragedy is when a person remains a spiritual baby or infant throughout their life. Could you imagine a 50-year-old person cradled in their mother's arms still nursing? That would be repulsive! In the same way, when we remain spiritual babies, it's just as bad.

Unfortunately, today, we don't really focus on spiritual maturity because we don't understand what it is and we haven't been challenged to attain it. While it should be a believer's highest goal in life, for many it's not even on their radar screen and something they're seriously pursuing.

Chapter 12

The Cost of the True Riches of Life

I wish I could say that acquiring the true riches of life was easy, but that would be deceptive. There's a cost to them, and we must make a conscious decision to pay the price to attain them.

In our day, there are many competing voices that tell us the true riches of life aren't worth it or aren't true. Ultimately, we must make that decision, and only we can make it. Many claim the true riches are wealth, popularity, happiness, and so on. We must decide whether we'll follow the values of those around us or those of God. And even if we do choose to consciously pursue the true riches of life, we must understand that following through will take a daily focus and thoughtful effort. In other words, we won't attain the true riches of life accidentally.

Discipleship Is How We Attain the True Riches of Life

Discipleship puts into place self-disciplines that provide the structure, on a long-term basis, for acquiring the true riches of life. It incorporates a system that will get us from point "A" to point "B."

What Is Discipleship?

Discipleship is the process of becoming like Christ in our nature, character, values, purposes, thoughts, knowledge, attitudes, and will. In other words, it's the process of becoming spiritually mature. It lasts a lifetime and isn't relegated to a temporary study or dedicated class taken for a time and then ended. Bill

Hull claims, "It's not a program or an event; it's a way of life. Discipleship is not for beginners alone; it's for all believers for every day of their lives."[27]

The Role of Discipleship in the Transformation Process

Discipleship is the vehicle God uses to build spiritual maturity in us. There is no other way! It's the pathway we must follow in order to be transformed into the image of Christ and attain all God intends us to be. Through discipleship, God grants us life, love, joy, peace, healthy minds, healthy relationships, healthy families, and healthy churches. It's our life's calling and the highest purpose to which we can give ourselves.

Howard Hendricks went so far as to claim, "When a person makes a profession of faith and … is never taken through a formal discipleship process, then there's little hope of seeing genuine spiritual transformation."[28]

To the degree we are committed to discipleship will be the degree to which we attain the true riches of life. To the degree we neglect our commitment to discipleship will be the degree to which we suffer destruction, devastation, and eternal loss.

---

[27] Bill Hull, *The Complete Book of Discipleship: On Being and Making Followers of Christ* (The Navigators Reference Library 1, 2014, NavPress, Kindle Edition), Kindle Locations 436-437.
[28] C. S. Lewis Institute, *Sparking a Discipleship Movement in America and Beyond,* cslewisinstitute.org, www.cslewisinstitute.org/webfm_send/210, Accessed 08/19/2016.

Modern Day Conveniences and the True Riches of Life

We live in an unparalleled time in the history of mankind. Advancements in technology have given us every modern convenience under the sun. While there are positives to these advancements, there are negatives as well. On the downside, in our effort to make life easier, we've become a soft and tender society. Toughness, suffering, hard work, endurance, self-discipline, and perseverance are lacking commodities.

My folks are from the Great Plain States of Nebraska and South Dakota. They grew up without electricity, indoor bathrooms, and running water in their homes. They had to walk or ride a horse to school, had no air conditioning during the hot, blistering summers, and had no heating throughout their uninsulated homes during the sub-zero winters. My mother tells of how she took a heated rock to bed at night to stay warm, and milked 26 cows before and after school. My father was extremely poor, worked hard, and was raised on side pork (the trash meat from pigs). He milked several cows twice daily and rode a horse 10 miles to school. My parents were tough, rugged, disciplined, hardworking folks who knew how to suffer and endure hardship, and it was the same for many others in their day as well.

I worry that because of our modern conveniences we've become spoiled. We know little about suffering hardship and going without. And when it comes to discipleship, instead of realizing that it requires discipline and toughness, we tend to do all we can to make it easy. We ask ourselves, "How can we make it fun, exciting, attractive, thrilling, and entertaining?"

It's just not realistic to think we can make the cost of discipleship that involves denying yourself, taking up your cross, losing your life, dying to self, hating your life, and being persecuted for Christ, convenient and entertaining. I fear we've become "lovers of pleasure rather than lovers of God," and we're trying to import our fun and entertainment syndrome into the discipleship-making process.

Discipleship Is Not Convenient

Today, if we have an inconvenience in our lives, we tend to buy something to fix it or take a pill to make us feel better. About the only thing left today that requires much hardship in life is sports. Other than that, almost everything else is convenient and easy. Unfortunately, the side effects of our conveniences are producing a soft and fragile society.

I believe our modern conveniences are also affecting our Christian lives. We don't like to be inconvenienced. We like instant gratification, ease, fun, and entertainment. Without realizing how much we've become products of our culture, deep within our subconscious mind is the belief that if something is hard we need to find a way to alleviate it.

Unlike what many would like, this attitude doesn't apply to discipleship and the Christian life. There's a cost to discipleship, and it's not convenient! It takes self-discipline, commitment, toughness, endurance, patience, and long-suffering. There's just no modern convenience that can make discipleship easy. We can't throw Christians in the microwave for a few minutes and pop out mature believers. Discipleship had a cost during the time of Christ, and it has a cost today. It has never been, and it will never be, convenient!

Busyness: An Enemy of the True Riches of Life

People's lives are extremely occupied with countless activities and stimuli each day. In fact, many are addicted to it and it has become their god. Cath Martin reveals that, because of our modern-day busyness, many Christians are even trying to sustain their relationships with God while on the go: "In the face of busy lives, many evangelicals are doing faith 'on the go' and utilizing digital media to help them maintain their spiritual lives. A third of these busy Christians now use Bible apps, with daily devotional apps and the Book of Common Prayer app among the popular choices."[29]

Many Christians say they don't have time for the true riches of life because they're too busy, yet they have plenty of time for all their other activities. Why is this so? The stats show that it's because many Christians are saying no to Christ and the true riches of

---

[29] Cath Martin, *Evangelicals Admit Struggling to Find Time for Daily Bible Reading and Prayer*, 2016, Christianity Today, www.christiantoday.com/article/daily.bible.reading.and.prayer.is.a.struggle.for.many.evangelicals/36765.htm, Accessed 08/18/2016.

Chapter 12: The Cost of the True Riches of Life

life and saying yes to their own desires and plans. Putting God first is sacrificed, or eliminated, while other activities are kept intact and prioritized.

Adding to all the pleasure-oriented stimuli available to us today is the pursuit of wealth, power, and prestige that we believe bring pleasure and happiness. In many households, both father and mother are working long hours in order to have large homes, nice cars, good retirement, vacations, and a host of other pleasures money can bring. The time in which we live is marked by busyness and the motto of our day is activity.

Even though spending time with God and His Word is critical for growth in Christ, busyness distracts many away. A recent Barna Group survey reveals this startling fact: "Like all other forms of analog media, the Bible is pushed to the side in part because people are just too busy. Among those who say their Bible reading decreased in the last year, the number one reason was busyness: 40% report being too busy with life's responsibilities (job, family, etc.), an increase of seven points from just one year ago."[30]

Distractions in the Formative Years

As a former youth pastor, I remember the difficulty I had with some of my students. It was a struggle getting them to youth group, church, and discipleship

---

[30] Barna Group, *The State of the Bible: 6 Trends for 2014*, 2014, https://www.barna.org/barna-update/culture/664-the-state-of-the-bible-6-trends-for-2014#.VdNGKTZRGUk, Accessed 08/18/2016.

activities because they just didn't have the time. They were too busy with school, sports, and jobs. Youth group and discipleship were in competition with their other pursuits, and unfortunately, most of the time the spiritual activities lost out. Growth in Christ and acquiring the true riches of life just weren't as high a priority. The good things in their lives were in the way. And sadly, most of their parents supported them and made schooling, sports, and jobs a priority for them over youth group and discipleship.

I often felt like I was fighting a losing battle and was grieved by their lack of growth. I've been able to trace the lives of many of these youth over the past 30 or so years, and today, many of them who made God and discipleship a low priority have paid a heavy price. Some no longer even walk with the Lord. The eternal consequences of the busyness in their lives have been, and will always be, an enormous cost to them.

In order to grab their attention, I often threatened to give these students a spiritual grade — a grade like they received in school for classes they attended. After all, they earned grades in school for how well they performed. What if I gave them a spiritual grade to help them see how well they were doing spiritually? Unfortunately, many would have flunked out.

Today, the average student spends around 7–8 hours in school a day, an hour or two on homework, an hour or two on extracurricular activities like sports, and then some have jobs on top of it all. And of course, we can't leave out TV, video games, and social media.

Chapter 12: The Cost of the True Riches of Life

When do they have time for God? Their lives are so stuffed full of other activities that being a disciple of Christ and pursuing the true riches of life are shoved to the wayside.

The average person will spend a year or so in kindergarten, 12 years in primary and secondary education, and four years in college. During these years, the amount of time spent learning about earthly knowledge is astronomical. However, the time spent learning about biblical knowledge is minuscule and scarcely measurable in comparison. We've elevated secular knowledge to such a high degree that we feel justified in sacrificing eternal knowledge on its altar.

I believe God is in favor of us being responsible in school, but I can't help but think He's more concerned that we acquire eternal knowledge so we can build our lives on a solid foundation and attain the true riches of life.

Building Upside Down

In biblical times, secular knowledge was built upon the foundation of Scripture. Critical factors like character, honesty, respect, self-discipline, diligence, hard work, and responsibility formed the foundation upon which secular knowledge rested.

Today, we have it backward. We make secular knowledge the foundation of life and demote eternal, biblical knowledge as subservient. In other words, we build biblical knowledge on the foundation of secular knowledge instead of building secular knowledge on the foundation of biblical knowledge. We give secular knowledge priority and, if we have time, squeeze in a little Bible knowledge.

For example, how many parents "stress out" if their children don't spend time studying their Bible like they do if they don't spend time doing their homework? Most parents are responsible regarding their children's secular knowledge but irresponsible regarding their children's biblical knowledge! We're doing just the opposite of the biblical model and then wonder why our sons and daughters aren't serious about their relationships with Christ. We wonder why, according to Rainer Research, "approximately 70% of American youth drop out of church between the age of 18 and 22."[31] Moreover, the Barna Group estimates that "80% of those reared in the church will be 'disengaged' by the time they are 29."[32]

Our priorities are backward, and we're paying a high price. By elevating secular knowledge over biblical knowledge and discipleship, many parents are participating in damaging their children's spiritual future, which will have consequences, not only in this life but in eternity as well.

Today, we're building on a shallow foundation. Many are building their houses on the sand. The state of the family is in disarray, our lives are harried and

---

[31] Drew Dyck, *The Leavers: Young Doubters Exit the Church*, 2010, ChristianityToday.com, www.christianitytoday.com/ct/2010/november/27.40.html, Accessed 09/28/2016.
[32] Ibid., Accessed 09/28/2016.

scarred, we're busy going every direction under the sun, and much of the free time we do have is spent on pleasure and entertainment. I'm afraid the average Christian today is falling far short of what Christ calls us to be.

Many are more concerned about their careers than Christ, more concerned about their earthly home than their eternal home, more concerned about sports activities than godly activities, more concerned about secular knowledge than biblical knowledge, more concerned about their physical condition than their spiritual condition, and more concerned about their present life than their eternal life.

Getting Rid of Unnecessary Weights

Many Christians today need to lighten up! They have too many activities — even good ones — in their lives that are distracting them away from the true riches of life. Scripture calls these activities "weights." It says, *"Therefore, since we are surrounded by so great a cloud of witnesses, let us also lay aside every **weight**, and sin which clings so closely, and let us run with endurance the race that is set before us"* (Heb. 12:1).

In this verse, two things can deter us from our commitment to discipleship: sin and weights. Weights refer to the activities in life that are not bad but take away our time. God wants us to slim down in these areas so we can have more time for discipleship and attain the true riches of life.

When we give priority to the "weights" in our lives,

we have less time to give God our best. Consequently, we wind up giving God our leftovers: leftover time, leftover energy, and leftover service. When Christ called the original disciples, He didn't call them to give Him their leftovers. Today, Christ doesn't call us to give Him our leftovers either. He calls us to put Him first and give Him our best.

Distractions and the True Riches of Life

In 1 Corinthians 7, God reveals how He feels about all the distractions that take us away from Him and the true riches of life:

> ***But I want you to be free from concern.*** *One who is unmarried is concerned about the things of the Lord, how he may please the Lord; but one who is married is concerned about the things of the world, how he may please his wife, and his interests are divided . . . This I say for your own benefit; not to put a restraint upon you, but to promote what is appropriate and to **secure undistracted devotion to the Lord*** (1 Cor. 7:32-35, NASB).

In this passage, the Apostle Paul is promoting the benefits of singleness. While he clearly states in the context that marriage is honorable and desirable, he also highlights how God feels about the distractions of life that can draw us away from Him.

Christ gave a warning as well about the distractions of life that would affect many in the last days: *"But watch yourselves lest your hearts be weighed down with*

Chapter 12: The Cost of the True Riches of Life

*dissipation and drunkenness and **cares of this life**, and that day come upon you suddenly like a trap"* (Luke 21:34).

God desires that we would be free from the distractions and concerns of the world so we can focus more fully on Him and the true riches of life. I wonder how He feels about us today?

A Lifelong Commitment to the True Riches of Life

God's will for us is that we would be fully devoted to acquiring the true riches of life. In so doing, we'll reap an eternal harvest we'll enjoy forever. However, by neglecting the true riches of life, we'll reject God's best for us and be bitterly disappointed someday.

We must understand that pursuing the true riches of life is not necessarily fun. Denying yourself is not a great thrill. Taking up your cross is not that exciting. Losing your life for the cause of Christ is not the latest fad. Suffering family division because of Christ is painful. Being ridiculed by society for holding to biblical truth is hard. Training yourself in godliness is not popular. Exercising self-discipline for the purpose of discipleship takes patience and fortitude. Not following the winds of modern-day morality is challenging. Reading the Bible instead of watching TV takes strong resolution. Praying requires commitment and patience, and losing friends because of Christ is lonely.

However, these challenges are the core principles for attaining the true riches of life that will bring us deep, genuine joy and eternal rewards in heaven. Those who are wise will choose the eternal riches over the fleeting pleasures of our day. They will be like Moses who, *"When he was grown up, refused to be called the son of Pharaoh's daughter, choosing rather to be mistreated with the people of God than to **enjoy the fleeting pleasures of sin***" (Heb. 11:24–25).

Are You Preparing for Your Departure?

Sometimes we're so invested in this life that we're overlooking the true riches of life and eternity. We're like a story told by Steven Cole:

> In 1981, a man was flown into the remote Alaskan wilderness to photograph the natural beauty of the tundra. He had photo equipment, 500 rolls of film, several firearms, and 1,400 pounds of provisions. As the months passed, the entries in his diary, which at first detailed the wonder and fascination with the wildlife around him, turned into a pathetic record of a nightmare. In August, he wrote, "I think I should have used more foresight about arranging my departure. I'll soon find out." He waited and waited, but no one came to his rescue. In November, he died in a nameless valley, by a nameless lake, 225 miles northeast of Fairbanks. An investigation revealed that he had carefully provided for his adventure, but he had made no

Chapter 12: The Cost of the True Riches of Life

provision to be flown out of the area.[33]

What a tragedy! This man prepared for everything but his departure. His story applies to us today. We can be so absorbed in this life that we're neglecting the true riches of life. We're substituting this life's temporal treasures for the eternal, true riches of life. And in so doing, we're forgetting that soon we'll be departing this life and leaving what we worked so hard to accumulate, behind.

It's only the true riches of life that we'll take with us into eternity. For this reason, Christ says, *"**Do not lay up for yourselves treasures on earth**, where moth and rust destroy and where thieves break in and steal, **but lay up for yourselves treasures in heaven**, where neither moth nor rust destroys and where thieves do not break in and steal. For where your treasure is, there your heart will be also"* (Matt. 6:19–21).

---

[33] Steven J. Cole, *Why You Should Hate Your Life*. Bible.org. 2014, bible.org/seriespage/lesson-67-why-you-should-hate-your-life-john-1224-26, Accessed 08/11/2016.

Bibliography

Baker, Greg S. *How to Build Good Character*. SelfGrowth.com. www.selfgrowth.com/articles/how_to_build_good_character. Accessed 12/14/2016.

Barna Group. *The State of the Bible: 6 Trends for 2014*. 2014. https://www.barna.org/barna-update/culture/664-the-state-of-the-bible-6-trends-for-2014#.VdNGKTZRGUk. Accessed 08/18/2016.

Beeksma, Deborah. *The Average Christian Prays a Minute a Day; Prayer by the Faithful Helps Their Relationships*. GodDiscussion.com. 2013. http://www.goddiscussion.com/110131/the-average-christian-prays-a-minute-a-day-prayer-by-the-faithful-helps-their-relationships. Accessed 07/27/2016.

Bible Hub. *703. Arête*. http://biblehub.com/greek/703.htm. Accessed 10/23/2016.

Blue Letter Bible. BlueLetterBible.org. *Study Resources: Charts and Quotes*. www.blueletterbible.org/study/pnt/pnt08.cfm. Accessed 10/14/16.

Character-training.com/blog. *What Is Character?* http://www.character-training.com/blog. Accessed 10/23/2016.

Christian Prayer Quotes. *Prayer Quotations*. http://www.christian-prayer-quotes.christian-attorney.net. Accessed 10/20/2016.

Cole, Steven J. *Why You Should Hate Your Life.* Bible.org. 2014. bible.org/seriespage/lesson-67-why-you-should-hate-your-life-john-1224-26. Accessed 08/11/2016.

C. S. Lewis Institute. *Sparking a Discipleship Movement in America and Beyond.* cslewisinstitute.org. http://www.cslewisinstitute.org/webfm_send/210. Accessed 08/19/2016.

Dyck, Drew. *The Leavers: Young Doubters Exit the Church.* 2010. ChristianityToday.com. www.christianitytoday.com/ct/2010/november/27.40.html. Accessed 09/28/2016.

Gotquestions.org. *What Does the Bible Say About Attitude?* www.gotquestions.org/Bible-attitude.html. Accessed 11/07/2016.

Hull, Bill. *The Complete Book of Discipleship: On Being and Making Followers of Christ.* The Navigators Reference Library 1. 2014. NavPress. Kindle Edition.

Issler, Klaus. *Six Themes to Guide Spiritual Formation Ministry Based on Jesus' Sermon on the Mount.* Source: Christian Education. Journal Date: September 1, 2010. CEJ: Series 3, Vol. 7, No. 2. ATLA Religion Database with ATLASerials. Hunter Resource Library. Accessed 11/5/2016.

Martin, Cath. *Evangelicals Admit Struggling to Find Time for Daily Bible Reading and Prayer.* 2014. Christianity Today. www.christiantoday.com/article/daily.bible.reading.and.prayer.is.a.struggle.for.many.evangelicals/36765.htm. Accessed 08/18/2016.

Bibliography

McGrath, Alister. *The Passionate Intellect; Christian Faith and the Discipleship of the Mind.* Source: Pro Ecclesia. 22 no 1 Winter 2013. Publication Type: Review ATLA Religion Database with ATLASerials. Hunter Resource Library. Accessed 11/5/2016.

Mohler, Albert, R. Jr. *The Scandal of Biblical Illiteracy: It's Our Problem.* Christianity.com. http://www.christianity.com/1270946. Accessed 08/18/2016.

Rankin, Russ. *Study: Bible Engagement in Churchgoer's Hearts, Not Always Practiced.* Nashville. 2012. http://www.lifeway.com/Article/research-survey-bible-engagement-churchgoers. Accessed 07/23/2016.

Statistic Brain Research Institute. *Television Watching Statistics.* 2015. www.statisticbrain.com/television-watching-statistics. Accessed 08/07/2016.

Swindoll, Chuck. *Strengthening Your Grip.* Waco, TX. Word Books. 1982.

Whitney, Donald S. *Spiritual Disciplines for the Christian Life.* Colorado Springs, Colorado. NAVPRESS. 1991.

Wilke, Jon D. *Churchgoers Believe in Sharing Faith, Most Never Do.* LifeWay.com. LifeWay Research. http://www.lifeway.com/article/research-survey-sharing-christ-2012. Accessed 08/04/2016.

About the Author

Todd M. Fink is founder and director of Go Missions to Mexico Ministries. He received a Bachelor of Theology Degree from Freelandia Bible College (1986-1990), did studies at Western Seminary (1990-1993), received a Master of Theology Degree from Freedom Bible College and Seminary (2012-2013), and received a Ph.D. degree in theology from Trinity Theological Seminary (2015).

He served as youth/associate pastor for 12 years at an Evangelical church in Oregon (1987-1998).

Todd (Mike) is currently serving as pastor and missionary with Go Missions to Mexico Ministries in Mexico (1998-present) and is also an author, speaker, and teacher. He has a deep passion for God's Word and enjoys helping people understand its eternal truths. He is married to his lovely wife, Letsy Angela, and has four grown children.

Connect with Todd (Mike)

Email: missionstomexico@yahoo.com

Facebook: Todd Mike Fink

Facebook Ministry Page: Go Missions to Mexico

Websites:

- ToddMichaelFink.com
- SelahBookPress.com
- GoMissionsToMexico.com
- HolyLandSite.com
- MinsiteriosCasaDeLuz.com

Ministries of Go Missions to Mexico

GoMissionsToMexico.com

HolyLandSite.com

MinisteriosCasaDeLuz.com

SelahBookPress.com

ToddMichaelFink.com

Look for More Books by Todd (Mike)

- *Biblical Discipleship: Essential Components for Attaining Spiritual Maturity*
- *Biblical Discipleship: Essential Components for Attaining Spiritual Maturity Study Guide*
- *Amazed: A Journey of Miracles*
- *Biblical Sites of the Holy Land: See Where the Bible Took Place*
- *Understanding the Fear of the Lord: How to Receive God's Richest Blessings in Your Life*
- *Understanding Heavenly Rewards: An Overlooked Truth*
- *Biblical Leadership: How to Lead God's Way*
- *Gender Roles in the Family and Church: What Does the Bible Say?*
- *Church Discipline: Intensive Care for Wayward Believers*
- *How to Share Your Faith: A Biblical Approach*

www.ingramcontent.com/pod-product-compliance
Lightning Source LLC
Chambersburg PA
CBHW021148080526
44588CB00008B/262